Lon;

GW01071872

Fourteen Stories

The translators:

David Richards, Reader in Russian at the University of
Exeter, is the author of several books on Russian life and
literature, and editor of *The Penguin Book of Russian Short
Stories* (1981).

Sophie Lund's previous translations from Russian have
been published by John Calder.

IVAN BUNIN

Long Ago

Fourteen stories translated by
David Richards and Sophie Lund

with an Introduction by David Richards

ANGEL BOOKS
LONDON

First published 1984 by Angel Books, 3 Kelross Road,
London N5 2QS

British Library Cataloguing in Publication Data

Bunin, I.A.
  Long ago : selected stories.
  I. Title
  891.73'42[F]   PG3476.B785

  ISBN 0-946162-10-7
  ISBN 0-946162-11-5 Pbk

Produced for the Publisher by
Alan Sutton Publishing Limited, Gloucester
Printed in Great Britain

Contents

Translators' Note

The translations in this volume reflect much amicable collaboration. The work was divided as follows: Sophie Lund translated *Chang's Dreams, Temir-Aksak-Khan, Long Ago, An Unknown Friend, At Sea, at Night, Sunstroke, The Caucasus, Visiting Cards* and *Zoyka and Valeria*; David Richards translated *The Primer of Love, Mitya's Love, Late Hour, The Riverside Tavern* and *A Cold Autumn*. We checked each other's drafts and together resolved a number of recurring difficulties. Our publisher Antony Wood then read through our versions and made many valuable suggestions, especially in regard to English style. Every translation has thus passed under three pairs of critical eyes. At the end of the day, however, final responsibility for each of these fourteen stories rests with the original translator.

D.J.R.
S.L.

Introduction

Life should be a delight.

BUNIN: *Arsenev's Life* (1933)

Ivan Bunin (1870–1953) is one of Russia's supreme literary artists, yet even now – more than fifty years after he was awarded the Nobel Prize for Literature – the unique power of his strikingly individual voice has not gained anything like due recognition in the English-speaking world. Indeed, the present volume is the first new edition of his stories to be published in English in the West for thirty-five years.

This neglect, however, would seem a not unexpected sequel to a life marked throughout by uncertainties and deprivations. After a happy childhood and youth on his parents' estates in Central Russia Bunin resolved in 1895 to devote himself to a full-time literary career. From then on his financial position was insecure and this, together with his penchant for a nomadic existence, meant that for many years he possessed no permanent home. On top of this he suffered first a long and tortured affair and then a disastrous marriage, the collapse of which was followed by the death of his only child at the age of five.

His early literary endeavours met with encouraging success. Between 1902 and 1909 Gorky's publishing house, Znaniye, issued five volumes of his work, he was three times awarded the Academy of Sciences' Pushkin medal for his poetry, and in 1910 he achieved popular acclaim for his long story of life in the Russian countryside, *The Village*. Not until he was in his mid-forties, however, did Bunin produce his first prose masterpieces, two of which, *The Primer of Love* (1915) and *Chang's Dreams* (1916), open the present volume. Just when his literary position seemed assured, the Revolutions of 1917 provoked a fresh crisis in his life. Once it became clear that the Bolsheviks would be victorious in the civil war, Bunin emigrated from Russia, never to return. In 1920, at the age of fifty, he had to start a new life and literary career in Western Europe.

Astonishingly, this was when his genius came into full flower. In a golden decade of creativity he proceeded to produce a seemingly endless stream of movingly eloquent short stories and also two longer works, *Mitya's Love* and his Proustian fictional autobiography, *Arsenev's Life*. Six masterly stories from this period are included in the present selection: *Temir-Aksak-Khan* (1921), *Long Ago* (1922), *An Unknown Friend* (1923), *At Sea, at Night* (1923), *Mitya's Love* (1924) and *Sunstroke* (1925).

Outside a small set of Russian émigré admirers, however, Bunin's superb post-revolutionary work was tragically ignored during his lifetime. In the Soviet Union he was condemned as a traitor and after 1928 nothing of his was published there until after his death. Few Western European *literati* knew Russian, and the translations of his works which occasionally appeared were either grossly inaccurate or completely insensitive, or both. Bunin's fortunes, both literary and financial, were given a welcome boost when he was awarded the Nobel Prize for Literature in 1933, but the benefits from this triumph were short-lived and soon completely extinguished by the Second World War which Bunin endured in Grasse, in the South of France, in a state of considerable deprivation.

The final disappointment of his life came when even his Russian émigré supporters turned away: his last volume of stories, *Dark Avenues* which was published in full in Paris in 1946 (eleven of the stories had been issued in New York three years earlier in a limited edition) was met with either silence or expressions of dismay at what were regarded as distasteful descriptions of sexual encounters. Bunin had cherished high hopes for this volume which he more than once claimed as his best work. Every one of the thirty-eight stories in *Dark Avenues* is about love, and although they almost all end unhappily their overall effect on the reader is not in the least dispiriting since the protagonists' experiences are recounted with such confident gratitude and delight. Six stories from this volume – *The Caucasus, Late Hour, Visiting Cards, Zoyka and Valeria, The Riverside Tavern* and *A Cold Autumn* – conclude the present collection.

Like most of the great Russian realists he admired, Turgenev, Chekhov and, above all, Tolstoy, Bunin drew artistic inspiration from his personal experience. Hence his stories are set for the most part in the late nineteenth- and early twentieth-century Russia he knew in his youth, but also in the France where he spent the last thirty years of his life, and in those countries of the Middle and Far East which he visited in the early years of the century.

Bunin's characters too are based on people he encountered – men and women of all sorts and conditions, foreigners as well as Russians. By his own account the first of his impulses as a writer was the realist's traditional determination to record for posterity as graphically as he could the solid material reality of the places and people of his time, which he consciously schooled himself to observe with the closest attention.

Many of his human records, though, remain external portraits – wonderfully firm, clear outlines, but with only hints of an inner life. Those of Bunin's characters who do reveal their innermost thoughts and feelings tend to be variations of a single type – a modern man, or more rarely woman, with a reflective turn of mind, finely tuned emotions, knowledge of the world and a capacity for wonder. This is no accident, for when it comes to psychology Bunin is not concerned to depict a variety of human reactions but rather to present to the reader the only psychological reality he is fully cognisant of, namely his own. 'A real artist,' he stated in an article of 1928 giving advice to young writers, 'always speaks primarily about his own soul.' Bunin's art is markedly egocentric: what he communicates is not an analysis of society together with a moral, political or religious message *à la* Tolstoy, Dostoyevsky or socialist realism, but a particular emotional response to the world, a response which remains remarkably consistent throughout his long career.

The most fundamental element in Bunin's view of life is a vivid sense of the precariousness of existence, an omnipresent awareness of the impermanence of all human constructions, achievements and hopes, a constant recognition that everything we value can be snatched away at any moment. As he wrote in the diary of his voyage to Ceylon just before the First World War:

> Over and over again I reflect: what a strange and terrible thing our life is – you are hanging by a thread every second. Here I am, alive and healthy, but who knows what may happen a second later to my heart, which, like every human heart, is unique in the whole of creation in its mysteriousness and fragility. And on just such a thread hang also my happiness and peace, that is the life and health of all those I love and whom I cherish much more than myself . . .

It was only natural that Bunin's post-emigration work should possess an elegiac quality, but even before the Bolshevik revolution destroyed so much that he cherished, the aristocratic Bunin and his heroes nostalgically mourned the loss of the Russian past, and examples of the ravages of time – from individual deaths to derelict country estates and the passing of whole civilizations – appear again and again even in his early pages. Ecclesiastes' lament, 'Vanity of vanities, all is vanity', echoes through Bunin's writing and in his protagonists' hearts and heads from the very beginning.

Yet this sense of precariousness and futility does not lead to despair. Quite the contrary, since it is those people with the keenest awareness of death, Bunin intimates, who paradoxically possess also the greatest capacity for joy and the most vivid appreciation of what for him was of supreme importance, namely those private experiences of awe, wonder or rapture that stir a man to the depths of his emotional being and leave an indelible mark on his spiritual consciousness. Bunin's second and most distinctive impulse as a writer was to depict precisely these experiences – experiences which together constitute what he would call *the poetry of life*. All his principal characters are sensitive to this poetry and it is their experiences of it that form the centre and meaning of every Bunin story.

Bunin's characters experience poetic emotions in various recurring situations. Over and over again they are moved by the beauty of the created universe: awe-struck by the grandeur of the heavens or by the surging power of the great oceans of the world, like the captain in *Chang's Dreams*; gently charmed by the Russian countryside, as is Ivlev, for instance, in *The Primer of Love*; or perhaps much more powerfully intoxicated by the burgeoning luxuriance of nature, like the young hero of *Mitya's Love*. Indeed, nowhere is Bunin's unique fusion of precise observation and sensual indulgence deployed more lavishly than in his depictions of spring and summer in this last extraordinary work.

Another frequent fount of poetic emotion is memory, which as early as 1916 Bunin described in *Chang's Dreams* as 'that God-given sight which none of us can understand.' The human memory, according to Bunin, not only helps us to make sense of our lives by sifting the significant events in our past from the insignificant, but, even more important, automatically transfigures and poeticizes the past which acquires then a certain legendary quality. Almost all Bunin's stories provide vivid illustrations of this process, as one character after another recalls emotionally vibrant incidents from his past, such as the two elderly passengers in *At Sea, at Night*, the narrators of *Late Hour* or *A Cold Autumn*, the doctor in *The Riverside Tavern* – and even the dog in *Chang's Dreams*! Often his narrators seem to be expressing his own nostalgia, as for example in *Long Ago* where we read of 'that sweet bitter dream of the past by which my soul will live until the grave', or in *Late Hour* which describes an old man's return to the little Russian town in the steppes which he has not seen since his early youth.

A special place in Bunin's poetry of life is occupied by sexual love, for although in this realm we may hope to enjoy the highest flights of rapture, we may also be driven as nowhere else to the blackest depths of despair. In many respects Bunin's approach to sex is surprisingly modern. His heroes are for instance in an almost perpetual state of erotic expectancy. It is not only the young hero of *Mitya's Love* who is looking for 'that legendary world of love which he had secretly been awaiting since childhood.' Bunin's older men too have constantly appreciative eyes for the slender waist, the neat ankle above an elegant shoe, the transparent white blouse or the coquettishly veiled face. Nor does Bunin shy away from describing nakedness – from Katya's innocent bosom early in *Mitya's Love* to the tiny, pear-shaped breasts, thin ribs, generous hips and luxuriant hair of the girl in *Visiting Cards*. Occasionally he even unexpectedly titillates the reader, as for instance when this same girl in *Visiting Cards* is described deriving further erotic stimulation from her awareness that other people are passing by only inches away from where she is lying with her lover, or when the chubby Zoyka in *Zoyka and Valeria* tricks her companion into kissing her bared behind.

This seemingly carefree attitude, however, which curiously anticipates the permissiveness of the decade after Bunin's death, is not the whole picture. 'Love is no simple episode in our lives', reads Ivlev, the hero of *The Primer of Love* in the ancient volume from which the story takes its title, and indeed, for Bunin the consequences of love (or even of a brief sexual encounter, as in

Sunstroke) may be not only profound and enduring, but even ultimately destructive. In story after story, sexual entanglements drive Bunin's characters to desolation, madness or self-destruction. An older-fashioned and deeper morality than permissiveness seems to dictate that in this area of poetic experience rapture has to be paid for, and we are reminded, more forcibly than elsewhere, of our fundamental human fragility.

Bunin provides his most detailed analysis of sexual derangement in *Mitya's Love*, a Russian version of Goethe's *Werther*. Against the ironic background of a radiantly blossoming natural world he traces with penetrating insight the inexorable steps in a poetically inclined young man's descent from the joyful confidence of early love to nightmarish despair. This story, Bunin's only *novella*, is one of the most compelling accounts of disintegration in all modern literature.

For Bunin himself art, especially literature, was a constant source of delight. In *Arsenev's Life* he describes his own early recognition of his calling to poetry and his growing love for the literature of his native land. Later, he was often to cite with approval the words of his favourite Persian poet Saadi's characterization of the writer's lot: 'How excellent is the life spent in contemplating the beauty of the world and leaving after one the impress of one's soul.' Though Bunin rarely makes his fictional heroes literary men, he regularly introduces quotations from his favourite prose-writers and poets into his stories and often makes his characters sensitive to literature. Thus, the young hero of *Mitya's Love* sees his personal joys and fears reflected in the poems he reads in the family library, while in the fourteen hauntingly pathetic letters that form *An Unknown Friend* Bunin gives to the invisible writer's lady admirer some of his own firmest convictions about art.

When modern Russian critics and readers call Bunin 'the last of
the classics' they have in mind not only his nostalgic evocations of
pre-revolutionary Russian life, but also his manner of writing. In
his dignified way Bunin is one of the greatest stylists in the
Russian language.

In the first place, his Russian is musical. Like Turgenev and
Pasternak, he started his literary career as a poet and often
commented that he did not draw a sharp line between his verse
and his prose. The latter possesses of course not the regular
rhythms of poetry but a subtler melodiousness which neverthe-
less still induces the reader to speak it aloud. Bunin claimed that
prose, like verse, 'must be in a definite key' and spoke too about
the need to establish 'the general resonance' of a work.

Bunin's prose reflects the poet's sensitivity in two further ways,
in his keen eye for accurate detail and in his cool verbal precision.
All short-story writers rely on significant detail, but Bunin's
images are particularly sharp, both in his concise descriptions of,
say, a haze of pollen wafting over the fields, the moon turning
dark pavements into black lace or the peculiar gait of pigeons, and
in his vivid extended accounts of, for example, a sleazy inn (*The
Riverside Tavern*), the animated quayside at Eupatoria (*At Sea, at
Night*) or a Parisian funeral (*Late Hour*).

In a passage in *Arsenev's Life* Bunin commented on his own
extraordinarily keen senses:

> . . . my sight was such that I could see all seven stars of the Pleiad, my
> hearing could catch a marmot's whistle in the evening countryside
> nearly half a mile away, and I would become intoxicated by the smell
> of a lily-of-the-valley or of an old book . . .

No less miraculous than this gift was Bunin's enduring ability
throughout the thirty-three years of his life in emigration to recall
with striking clarity detail after detail of his early days in Russia.
Artists, he claimed, were distinguished by 'an especially vivid

and especially graphic sensory memory'. One of the most con-
vincing illustrations of this thesis is Bunin himself.

With all his linguistic genius Bunin never indulges in verbal
fireworks for their own sake. No matter how violent or lyrical his
subject-matter may be, his language remains cool, controlled and
precise – in other words classical. His early stories are more
ornate than the later ones, in some of which Bunin achieves a
fluent economy of diction rarely matched by any other Russian
writer. *A Cold Autumn*, for instance, using the simplest language,
conveys in a few brief pages all the pathos of war and revolution
and the pain and poetry of a woman's entire life. As the émigré
Russian critic Vladimir Weidlé put it, Bunin is fascinated above
all by 'the confident full weight of a sentence set firmly in its place
and riveted to the thought it expresses'. In this precision, which
gives a uniquely close attention to each word, claims Weidlé,
Bunin is superior even to Turgenev and Tolstoy.

Ironically, the refined grace of Bunin's Russian derives in part
from his very abandonment of his homeland after the Revolution.
Living in Western Europe, he was able to avoid not only the
political pressures of socialist realism but also the linguistic
changes wrought by communism. Even in his late writings his
language remains that of the nineteenth-century landed gentry,
now slightly old-fashioned, but possessing the poetic charm of a
lost golden age.

One of the distinguishing characteristics of modern Russian
literature – not only under the Soviet regime, but from about the
middle of the nineteenth century – is its moral earnestness and
the prominence given to social and political questions. Bunin,
however, is right outside this tradition. His characters express no
interest in the organization of society and say almost nothing
about either politics or morality. Bunin does not try to educate
his readers and, unlike his literary hero Tolstoy, he was never a

repentant nobleman striving to expiate his sense of guilt over his privileged position in pre-revolutionary Russian society. From the beginning Bunin was above all a literary craftsman whose first concern was to produce elegantly shaped works of art.

On top of this, his enjoyment of the 'poetry of life' and his hedonistic delight in the simpler pleasures of existence – food, drink, sunshine, good conversation, travel, flirtation – are so direct and are accompanied throughout by such an openly expressed sense of wonder at the splendour of it all that even the darker experiences in his fiction are embraced within a pervasive feeling of gratitude. Reading Bunin is always uplifting because his work, more convincingly than that of any other Russian writer except perhaps Pushkin, confirms Pasternak's assertion that 'art, even tragedy, is an account of the happiness of being alive.'

David Richards

The Primer of Love

Translated by David Richards

Ivlev was travelling once at the beginning of June over to the far side of his province.

The tarantass with its crooked, dusty roof had been lent by his brother-in-law, on whose estate he was spending the summer. The three horses, small but sturdy and with thick matted manes, he'd hired in the village from a rich peasant. The latter's son, a dull-witted but confident lad of about eighteen, was driving. He was ruminating discontentedly over something all the time, seemed somehow offended, and didn't understand jokes. So, realizing that there was no chance of any conversation with him, Ivlev gave himself over to that calm and aimless watching the world pass by which goes so well with the rhythm of hooves and the tinkling of halter-bells.

At first the journey was pleasant: it was a warm, dull day, the track had been worn smooth, and in the fields were masses of flowers and larks; a balmy breeze wafted over the corn and over the short, greyish-blue rye which extended as far as the eye could see; it was blowing pollen across the fields, puffing it up in places to form a sort of mist in the distance. The lad, wearing a new peaked cap and an ill-fitting lustrine jacket, sat erect; the fact that the horses had been completely entrusted to him and that he was all dressed up made him particularly serious. And the horses were coughing and trotting unhurriedly, with the swingle-tree of the left-hand horse now scraping against the wheel, now being jerked clear, while all the time the white steel of the worn horse-shoe glinted beneath it.

'Shall we stop at the count's?' asked the lad without turning round, as a village suddenly loomed up ahead of them, its willow-trees and an orchard masking the horizon.

'What for?' replied Ivlev.

The lad paused and then, flicking a fat gadfly off one of the horses with his whip, answered:

'To get a drink of tea.'

'It's not tea you're thinking about,' said Ivlev. 'You always feel sorry for the horses.'

'A horse doesn't worry about the journey, it worries about its food,' said the lad didactically.

Ivlev glanced around. The weather had deteriorated; faded-looking clouds had gathered on all sides and it was already drizzling – those unassuming days regularly end in rain . . .

An old man ploughing at the edge of the village said that only the young countess was at home, but they still stopped. The lad draped a heavy peasant's coat round his shoulders and, happy that the horses were now resting, sat calmly out in the rain on the box of the tarantass which had come to a halt in the middle of a dirty yard alongside a stone trough firmly embedded in the hoof-pitted ground. He kept examining his boots and adjusting the shaft-horse's breast-band with his whip-handle. Ivlev, on the other hand, was sitting in the drawing-room, which the rain was making darker and darker, chatting with the countess and waiting for tea. There was already a smell of burning woodshavings, and thick green smoke was drifting past the windows from a samovar which a bare-footed wench on the porch was filling with bundles of woodchips, which burnt with a bright red flame as she poured kerosene on them.

The countess was wearing a flowing pink tea-gown, which revealed her powdered neck. She was smoking, inhaling deeply, and constantly adjusted her hair, baring her firm round arms to the shoulder. Inhaling and laughing, she kept bringing the conversation round to love and amongst other things spoke about her near neighbour Khvoshchinsky, who, as Ivlev had known since he was a child, had all his life been unhinged by love for his maidservant Lushka who'd died very young.

'Ah, the legendary Lushka!' Ivlev commented jokingly, slightly embarrassed at his confession. 'Because that crank worshipped her and devoted his whole life to mad dreams about her I was almost in love with her myself in my youth, and used to imagine God knows what as I thought about her – though they do say she was quite ugly.'

'Yes?' said the countess, not listening. 'He died this winter. And Pisarev, the only person he allowed to visit him, for old time's sake, maintains that he wasn't at all unhinged in any other area, and I fully accept that – he just wasn't in tune with the people of today.'

At last, with extraordinary caution, the barefooted wench brought in an old silver tray with a glass of strong, greyish, pond-water tea and á little basket of fly-blown biscuits.

By the time they drove off the rain had become really heavy. Ivlev had to pull up the roof of the tarantass and sit huddled under the stiff, dried-out apron. The horses' bells were rattling, streams of water ran down their shiny dark haunches, the grass on the strip between the cornfields where the lad had driven as a short cut was swishing under the wheels, and beneath the roof the warm aroma of rye mingled with the smell of the old tarantass.

'So, there we are,' thought Ivlev, 'Khvoshchinsky is dead. We really must call in there, if only to peep at the mysterious Lushka's deserted shrine. But what sort of a man was this Khvoshchinsky? Was he mad, or just slightly touched, a mind obsessed with one single thing?' According to the older generation of landowners, Khvoshchinsky's contemporaries, he'd once had the reputation in the district for being an exceptionally clever fellow. And suddenly he'd been struck by this love, this Lushka, and then by her unexpected death – and everything had gone to pieces. He'd locked himself up in the house, in the room where Lushka lived and died, and spent more than twenty years sitting on her bed; he not only didn't go out, he didn't even show himself to anyone on his own estate. He wore out the mattress on Lushka's bed by sitting there all the time, and would ascribe to Lushka's influence literally everything that happened in the world: if a thunderstorm arose, Lushka had sent it; if war was declared, it meant that Lushka had decided it should be so; if the harvest failed, the peasants had displeased Lushka . . .

'It's Khvoshchinsky's you're going to, isn't it?' Ivlev shouted, sticking his head out into the rain.

'Yes, to Khvoshchinsky's,' the lad's voice echoed indistinctly through the rain; the water was running off his drooping cap. 'By Pisarev's hill.'

Ivlev didn't know that route. The region was looking increasingly remote and impoverished. The boundary strip came to an end, the horses slowed to a walk and pulled the tilting tarantass downhill along an eroded rut into some still unmown meadows whose green slopes stood out gloomily against the low clouds. Then the track, now disappearing, now appearing again, began to zigzag along the bottom of a series of ravines and through gulleys thick with alder and willow. They passed a small apiary with a few hives standing on a slope and some tall grass dotted red with wild strawberries. They drove round an old weir overgrown with nettles and a long dried-up pond, which had become a deep gulley full of weeds taller than a man – a pair of snipe flew screeching out of them up into the rainy sky. And on the weir, amid the nettles, stood a large old bush, one of those delightful southernwoods which are known as 'God's-trees', ablaze with its pale-pink blossom. And suddenly Ivlev recalled the area and remembered that in his youth he had ridden through there more than once . . .

'They say she drowned herself here,' said the lad unexpectedly.

'You mean Khvoshchinsky's mistress, I suppose?' asked Ivlev. 'It's not true, she never thought of drowning herself.'

'She did drown herself,' said the lad. 'And I think he most likely went off his head because he was poor rather than because of her.'

Then, after a short pause, he added gruffly:

'But we'll have to stop again . . . in that, in Khvoshchino, or whatever it's called. Look how tired the horses are!'

'Please do,' said Ivlev.

The track, now pewter-coloured from the rainwater, brought them to a knoll on which, in a clearing amidst wet rotting woodshavings and leaves, among tree-stumps and young aspen shoots with their fresh bitter smell, stood a solitary hut. There was no sign of life apart from a few yellow buntings which sat in the rain on some tall flowers and filled the entire sparse wood behind the hut with their song. But when the vehicle squelched through the mud and drew level with the hut, a whole pack of huge dogs, black, brown and smoky-grey, rushed out and surrounded the equipage with their furious barking, jumping right up at the horses' noses, turning round in the air and hurling themselves almost under the roof of the tarantass. At the same time, and just as unexpectedly, the sky above the tarantass was suddenly rent with a deafening thunder-clap, the lad frenziedly lashed at the dogs with his whip, and the horses took off at a gallop through the aspen stumps which flashed past their eyes . . .

The Khvoshchinsky estate was already visible beyond the wood. The dogs dropped behind, immediately fell silent and ran back purposefully; the wood opened out and ahead of them again lay open countryside. Evening was drawing in and it was impossible to tell whether the thunderclouds on three sides were dispersing or coming towards them. To the left the sky was almost black, though with patches of light blue; to the right it was grey and rumbled with incessant thunder; while to the west, beyond the Khvoshchinsky estate and the hillsides above the river valley, it was a dull dark-blue and trailed powdery-looking streaks of rain through which mountains of more distant clouds showed pink. Straight overhead, however, the rain was becoming lighter, and Ivlev, who was spattered all over with mud, stood up and with a feeling of pleasure pushed back the heavy roof of the tarantass to inhale the damp aromatic air of the countryside.

He fixed his eyes on the approaching estate and at last saw what he had heard so much about, though it still seemed to him as if Lushka had lived and died not twenty years before, but almost in times immemorial. Along the valley the trace of a shallow rivulet disappeared into the rushes and above it flew a white gull. Further on, midway up the hill, lay lines of hay which had turned dark in the rain; between them towered a number of widely-spaced silvery poplars. The house itself which was fairly large stood with its shabby white-washed walls and a shiny wet roof in a completely open space. There were no farm buildings or garden around it – just two brick pillars in place of a gate and masses of burdock in the ditches. When the horses forded the rivulet and climbed the hill, a woman in a man's light overcoat with sagging pockets was driving some turkeys through the burdock. The façade of the house was thoroughly featureless; it had very few windows and those that existed were small and set deep in the thick walls. Yet the gloomy porches were enormous. From one of these a young man wearing a grey school shirt belted with a broad strap was watching the approaching travellers. He was dark, had handsome eyes and was very personable, though his face was pale and bright with freckles, like a bird's egg.

They had to offer some explanation for their arrival. Mounting the porch and introducing himself, Ivlev said that he would like to examine and perhaps buy the library which according to the countess the deceased had left. The young man blushed a deep red and immediately led him into the house. 'So this is the son of the celebrated Lushka,' thought Ivlev, running his eyes over everything they passed, frequently turning to look at something and saying the first thing that came into his head just to be able to have another glance at the owner who seemed too young for his years. The latter answered hurriedly but monosylabically and became confused, evidently from a mixture of shyness and eagerness. That he was frightfully pleased at the prospect of selling some books and imagined they would fetch a high price was clear from his very first words, from the awkward haste with which he declared that no money could buy books like his. He led Ivlev through a semi-dark entrance hall whose floor was strewn with damp-reddened straw and into a large anteroom.

'Is this where your father lived?' asked Ivlev, taking off his hat as he entered.

'Yes, here,' the young man hastened to reply. 'That is, of course, not exactly here; you see, he spent most of his time sitting in the bedroom, but of course he also used this room . . .'

'Yes, I know; I realize he was ill,' said Ivlev.

The young man flared up.

'What do you mean, ill?' he said, and a more masculine note could be heard in his voice. 'That's all gossip. He wasn't at all ill mentally. He simply read all the time and didn't go out anywhere, that's all . . . No, please don't take your cap off, it's cold here; we don't live in this part of the house, you see.'

Indeed, it was much colder in the house than outside. In the unfriendly anteroom whose walls were papered with newspaper a bast quail-cage stood on the sill of a window gloomy from the clouds. On the floor a little grey bag was jumping about by itself. Bending down, the young man caught it and put it on a bench, and Ivlev realized that the quail was tied up in the bag. Then they went into the hall. This room with its windows facing north and west occupied almost half of the entire house. Through one window a centuries-old, completely black weeping-birch could be seen, standing out against the gold of the twilight sky which was growing clear beyond the thunderclouds. The front corner of the room was completely occupied by an unglassed shrine which was festooned with icons. Among them one icon in a silver casing stood out in both size and antiquity; on it lay a set of corpse-yellow wedding-candles bound with pale-green ribbons.

'Forgive me,' Ivlev began, trying to overcome his reticence, 'was your father . . .'

'No, not really,' muttered the young man, suddenly grasping his meaning. 'It was after she died he bought those candles and even started wearing a wedding ring all the time . . .'

The furniture in the hall was rough, but between the windows stood several beautiful cabinets full of tea services and tall slender goblets with gold rims. The floor was covered with dry bees which crunched underfoot. Also strewn with bees was the totally empty drawing-room. Passing through the latter and also through another gloomy room with a stove-bench, the young man stopped in front of a low door and took a huge key out of his trouser-pocket. Turning it with great difficulty in the rusty key-hole, he threw open the door, muttering something, and Ivlev saw a tiny room with two windows; against one wall stood a bare iron bedstead, and against the other two little book-cases of Karelian birch.

'So this is the library?' asked Ivlev, going up to one of them.

And the young man, hastening to answer in the affirmative, helped him to open the bookcases and began avidly to follow Ivlev's hands.

Very strange books made up that library! Ivlev opened the thick covers, turned back the rough grey pages and read: *Magic Landmarks; Morning Star and Nocturnal Demons; Reflections on the Mysteries of Creation; A Wonderful Journey to the Enchanted Land;* and *A Modern Book of Dreams.* And his hands trembled slightly. So this was the nourishment of that lonely heart which had locked itself away from the world for ever in this tiny room and only quite recently left it. But perhaps this heart had indeed not been quite mad?

'There is a realm' – Ivlev found himself recalling Baratynsky:

> 'There is a realm, though it has no name,
> Neither sleep nor waking, but between,
> Our mind, once there, will lose its frame,
> For the marches of madness it has seen.'

The sky in the west had cleared, and a golden light shone from behind the beautiful lilac-coloured clouds, strangely illuminating that poor refuge of love, that refuge of an incomprehensible love which had transformed into an enraptured martyrdom a whole human life which perhaps might have been destined to follow a quite ordinary course, had there not chanced to be a Lushka with her mysterious fascination . . .

Pulling a stool out from under the bedstead, Ivlev sat in front of the bookcase and took out his cigarettes, unobtrusively surveying the room and trying to commit it to memory.

'Do you smoke?' he asked the young man who was standing over him.

The latter blushed again.

'Yes,' he muttered and tried to smile. 'That is, I don't exactly smoke, I just treat myself occasionally. But – thank you – I'm very grateful.'

And clumsily taking a cigarette, he lit it with trembling hands, went over to the windowsill and sat on it, blocking out the yellow light of the sunset.

'And what's this?' asked Ivlev, bending down to the middle shelf on which lay a single very small book, rather like a prayer-book, and also a casket with corners edged in age-tarnished silver.

'It's . . . this casket has my mother's necklace in it,' answered the young man, faltering but trying to speak casually.

'May I look?'

'Of course, but it's a very plain one, you know, it wouldn't interest you.'

Opening the casket, Ivlev saw a worn string and a row of cheap, bright-blue beads which looked like stones. And at the sight of these beads which had once lain on the neck of the woman who was destined to be so adored and whose dim image could not but be beautiful, such a wave of emotion ran through him that palpitations made his eyes dance. When he had gazed at it for a while Ivlev carefully replaced the casket on the shelf. Then he turned to the little book. It was a tiny volume, charmingly produced a hundred years before, *A Primer of Love, or the Art of Loving and Being Loved.*

'That book, unfortunately, I can't sell.' The young man just managed to bring the words out. 'It's very precious . . . My father used to keep it under his pillow.'

'But perhaps you could let me just glance at it?' said Ivlev.

'Please do,' replied the young man in a whisper.

And overcoming his embarrassment, though somewhat disconcerted by the young man's fixed gaze, Ivlev began slowly to turn the pages of the primer of love. The whole volume was divided into short chapters: 'On Beauty', 'On the Heart', 'On the Mind', 'On Signs of Love', 'On Attack and Defence', 'On Disagreement and Reconciliation', 'On Platonic Love', etc. Each chapter comprised a number of short, elegant and at times very subtle maxims, some of which had been delicately underlined in red ink.

'Love is no simple episode in our lives,' read Ivlev.

'Our reason contradicts the heart, but does not convince it.'

'Women are never stronger than when they arm themselves with frailty.'

'We adore woman because she exercises sovereignty over our ideal dreams.'

'Vanity chooses; real love does not choose.'

'The beautiful woman must occupy second place; the first belongs to the loving woman. The latter becomes empress of our heart: before we realize it, our heart has become the slave of love for ever.'

Then came 'Interpretation of the Language of Flowers', and again certain items had been underlined:

'Wild poppy – sadness.'

'Spindletree – your charms are imprinted in my heart.'

'Periwinkle – sweet memories.'

'Geranium cinereum – melancholy.'

'Wormwood – eternal sorrow.'

And on a blank page at the very end a quatrain had been written in a minute neat hand and the same red ink; the young man craned his neck as he looked into the *Primer of Love* and said with a forced smile:

'He made that up himself.'

Half an hour later Ivlev bade him farewell with a sense of relief. Of all the books he had purchased only that tiny volume, and at a high price. The dull-golden sunset was fading in the clouds beyond the fields, casting its yellow reflection in the puddles; the fields were wet and green. The lad drove slowly, but Ivlev did not urge him on. The lad was explaining that the woman who'd earlier been driving the turkeys through the burdock was the deacon's wife and that the young Khvoshchinsky lived with her. Ivlev wasn't listening. He was still thinking about Lushka, and her necklace which had left a complex impression in him rather like that he had once experienced in a small Italian town after looking at the relics of a certain female saint. 'She's entered my life for ever!' he suddenly thought. And taking the *Primer of Love* out of his pocket, in the light of the sunset he slowly read again the lines written on the last page:

> 'Live by fair legends,'
> Say the wise men above,
> 'And bequeath to your scions
> This Primer of Love.'

Moscow, February 1915

Chang's Dreams

Translated by Sophie Lund

Does it really matter whose story this is? Every creature on earth deserves to have its story told.

One fine day Chang came to know the world and the Captain his master, with whom he shared his earthly existence. And since that time, six whole years have passed, running out like the grains of sand in a ship's hour-glass.

Now once again a night has come and gone: is it dream or reality? – and once again it's nearly morning: is it reality or only a dream? Chang is old and Chang is a drunkard – he's always dozing.

Outdoors in the city of Odessa, it's winter-time. The weather is fierce and gloomy, far worse even than on that day in China when Chang and the Captain first met. Powdery, razor-sharp snow is falling fast, swirling diagonally across the slippery asphalt of the deserted sea-front boulevard and lashing painfully at the face of every Jew who, hands in pockets and back hunched, goes scurrying awkwardly to the right or left. Beyond the harbour, which is also deserted, and the bay which is in a blur of snow, bare steppe is just discernible, running down to the shore. The pier steams, wreathed in clouds of dense grey smoke: from morning to night the sea, swollen with billowing foam, has been flooding over it. The wind whistles shrilly in the telephone wires.

On days like these, life doesn't begin early in the city. Nor are Chang and the Captain early risers. Six years – is it a long or a short time? In six years Chang and the Captain have become old men – although the Captain has yet to reach forty – and they've suffered a dramatic change of fate. They no longer sail the seas and live 'ashore', as sailors say, and not even where once upon a time they used to live, but in a narrow, rather dismal street in the attic of a five-story building which smells of coal and is inhabited by the kind of Jews who only return to the bosom of their families late in the evening and sit down to supper with hats on the back of their heads. The ceiling of Chang and the Captain's present home is low and their room is large and cold. Furthermore, it is always dark here because the two windows set into the sloping wall under the eaves are small and round and reminiscent of portholes. Something that vaguely resembles a chest-of-drawers stands between these windows, and an old iron bedstead leans against the left-hand wall: and that completes the appointments of this melancholy abode, not counting the fireplace which blows a constant draught of cold air into the room.

Chang sleeps in a little corner behind the fireplace and the Captain on the bed. The appearance of this bed, which sags almost all the way to the floor, and the condition of its mattress can easily be imagined by anyone who has ever lived in an attic, while the grubby pillow is so flat that the Captain finds it necessary to place his jacket beneath it. Nevertheless, even on a bed such as this the Captain sleeps very peacefully – lying flat on his back with his eyes closed and his face ashen, as motionless as a dead man. What a magnificent bed he once had! Handsome and high with fitted drawers and deep cosy bedding, fine slippery sheets and cool, snow-white pillows! But in those days, even when he was being rocked by the sea, the Captain never slept so soundly: now he finds the day very tiring, and what is there to trouble him, what can there be that he must not sleep through, and what possible joy can the new day bring? At one time there were two truths in the world, endlessly revolving in his mind: the first was that life was unutterably beautiful, and the second that life was only to be contemplated by madmen. Now the Captain insists that there is, and was, and forever and ever will be, only one truth – the latter, the truth that belongs to the Jew Job and to the wise man from that mysterious tribe, Ecclesiastes. These days, sitting in the beer parlour, the Captain will often pronounce: 'Remember now thy Creator in the days of thy youth, while the evil days come not, nor the years draw nigh, when thou shalt say, I have no pleasure in them.' But the days and the nights still exist in the same old way and once again a night has come and gone and once again it's nearly morning. And Chang and the Captain wake up.

However, having awakened, the Captain doesn't open his eyes. At this moment even Chang who is lying on the floor near the empty fireplace, which all night has been filled with the fresh breath of the sea, doesn't know what's in his mind. The only thing that Chang knows for sure is that the Captain won't move for at least an hour. He glances at him out of the corner of one eye, lowers his lids and drifts back to sleep. Chang, too, is a drunkard and also feels giddy and weak in the morning, perceiving the world through that sullen haze of disgust which is so familiar to anyone who has ever been on board ship and suffered from sea-sickness . . . And so, as he dozes through these early hours, Chang's sleep is filled with leaden, oppressive dreams . . .

In his dream:

An old, sour-faced Chinaman had climbed up onto the deck of the steamer and crouching down on his haunches begun to whine, imploring everyone who walked past to buy the little basket of rotting fish which he had brought with him. It was a cold and dusty day on the broad Chinese river. Beneath the rush sail of a boat rocking on the river's muddy swell sat a puppy – a little ginger dog with his ears cocked, a hint of fox or wolf about him and a stiff collar of thick fur around his neck – surveying the high wall of the ship's iron side with black, stern, intelligent eyes.

'Why don't you sell me the dog instead?' the young captain of the vessel shouted from where he was standing idly in his turret, loudly and merrily, as if the Chinaman were deaf.

The Chinaman, Chang's first master, raised his eyes and, dumbfounded both by the shout and his own good fortune, began bowing and lisping in English: 'Ve'y good dog, ve'y good!' Thus, for the sum of just one rouble, the pup changed hands, acquired the name of Chang, and in the company of his new master set sail that very same day for Russia – and at first, for three long weeks, was so desperately sea-sick and in such a daze that he failed to notice anything: not even the ocean, or Singapore, or Colombo.

It was the beginning of the Chinese autumn and the weather was rough. Chang began to feel ill as soon as they came out into the estuary. The rain drove towards them out of the murk, the watery plain sparkled with white-caps, and the greeny-grey jagged swell raced and heaved and splashed aimlessly as the flat shores on either side drew further apart and disappeared into the fog – and there was more and more water all around. Chang in his silvery rain-soaked coat and the Captain in his hooded oilskins stood on the bridge, which felt even higher than before. The Captain issued commands while Chang trembled, and turning his muzzle this way and that, tried to escape the wind. The water was expanding, embracing the bleak horizons and mingling with the murky sky. Snatching drops of moisture from the broad, seething swell, the wind rushed in as it pleased, whistled through the ship's rigging, and slapped and boomed down below against the canvas awnings which the sailors in boots and wet rain-capes were struggling to release, catch and stow away. Eager to find the most effective place from which to strike, it waited until the ship, bowing slowly before it, had made a sharp turn to starboard, and then lifted her up onto the back of such a towering, furiously boiling roller that she couldn't hold on and came crashing down the other side, burrowing deep into the surf, while in the chart-house a coffee cup, left on the table by one of the stewards, suddenly flew to the floor with a ringing, shattering sound . . . And then the fun began!

All kinds of weather came after this: now the sun would burn

like a flame from out of a radiant azure sky, now clouds would
gather like mountain peaks and reverberate with peals of terrify-
ing thunder, now tumultuous rain-storms would pelt down upon
both ship and sea: but the pitching and rolling never ceased, even
when they were standing still. For three whole weeks, Chang,
tortured beyond endurance, never once managed to leave his
corner in the stuffy, half-dark corridor on the quarter-deck,
where surrounded by empty second-class cabins he lay close to
the high threshold of the door which led out onto the deck and
was opened only once every twenty-four hours for the Captain's
orderly to bring Chang his food. And Chang was left with
nothing to remember of that entire journey to the Red Sea save
for the heavy creaking of partitions, the nausea, and the thud of
his wildly beating heart hurtling down into some kind of abyss
with the shuddering stern of the ship before being lifted high into
the sky, and the prickly sensation of mortal terror as that same
stern, flying skywards and then suddenly crashing down on its
side, screws roaring in thin air, was all of a sudden assailed by a
whole mountain of water which burst upon it with the fury of
cannon-fire, first dousing the daylight in the bullseye panes of the
portholes and then streaming down their thick glass in cloudy
torrents. The sick Chang heard commands being shouted in the
distance, the ear-splitting whistle of the boatswain, the clatter of
sailors' feet somewhere above his head, the noise of rushing,
bubbling water, and, peering through half-closed lids at the
shadowy corridor stacked with bales of tea wrapped in sacking,
lay in a drunken stupor from the heat, the nausea and the pungent
smell of tea . . .

But here Chang's dream is interrupted.

Chang wakes with a start and opens his eyes: it's no longer a
wave hitting the stern, but the sound of a door being slammed
loudly somewhere downstairs. And now, noisily, the Captain
clears his throat and begins to rise slowly from his sagging couch.
He pulls on his battered shoes, ties their laces, puts on the black

gold-buttoned tunic which he has fished out from under his pillow, and makes his way to the chest-of-drawers while Chang, in his shabby little ginger coat, gives a yelp and a brief querulous yawn and gets up from the floor. On the chest-of-drawers stands an opened bottle of vodka. The Captain takes a swig and then, slightly out of breath and puffing into his whiskers, goes over to the fireplace and pours a little vodka into the bowl standing beside it, so that Chang too may have his share. Chang begins to lap greedily and the Captain, lighting a cigarette, goes back to bed to await the time when the morning will begin in earnest. Already, the distant rumble of trams can be heard and already, from far below, comes the continuous clatter of horses' hoofs on the street outside, but it is still too early to get up. So the Captain stays in bed, smoking. And, having finished his bowl, Chang also lies down. He jumps onto the bed, curls up in a ball at the Captain's feet, and gradually sinks into that blissful state which vodka always brings. His half-closed eyes mist over and, gazing feebly at his master with a feeling of growing tenderness, he thinks a thought which if he were a human being could be expressed something like this: 'Oh, you fool, you fool! There's only one truth in the world, and if you only knew what a sublime truth it is!' And again, floating back into his dreams, or his half-awake thoughts, comes that distant morning when the ship, sailing from China with Chang and the Captain aboard, left the tormented, turbulent waters of the ocean and entered the Red Sea.

In his dream:

Once past Perim, the ship began to swing more and more lazily until she was rocking like a cradle, and Chang fell into a sweet, deep slumber. Then suddenly, having awoken with a start, he felt the most profound amazement: everything around him was quiet and peaceful, the stern was humming evenly, no longer plunging into space, the water murmured gently, streaming by somewhere on the other side of the walls, and the warm aroma of food drifting in under the door leading to the deck was enchanting . . . Chang raised himself onto his front paws and peered into the empty passengers' lounge: there in the half-light, he saw the soft gleam of something that was a golden lavender colour, something hardly visible to the naked eye, but full of unbeliev-able joy – the rear portholes stared wide-open into a blue sunlit void, into space and air, while rivers of mirrored light ran in sinuous, never-ending streams across the low ceiling. And Chang had an experience that in those days his master the Captain often had as well: he suddenly realized that the world contained not one truth, but two: first, that to live on this planet and to sail its seas was appalling, and second . . . But Chang had no time to ponder on the second truth: all of a sudden the door flew open to reveal the ladder leading up to the spar-deck, the black glistening mass of the ship's funnel, and the sky of a radiant summer morning, while emerging from under the ladder, from out of the engine room, came the swiftly approaching figure of the Captain, dressed in crisp white from head to toe, freshly scrubbed and shaved and exuding the cool scent of cologne, his sandy whiskers groomed to raised points in the German fashion, his piercing pale eyes brimming with light. And at the sight of all this Chang gave such a joyous leap forward that the Captain, catching him in mid-flight, planted a kiss on the top of his head, and turning back with him in his arms, was up the ladder to the spar-deck and the upper-deck in three bounds, then sprang even higher onto that same bridge where in the estuary of the great Chinese river Chang had known such terror.

On the bridge, the Captain went into the chart-house while Chang, who had been dropped onto the deck, sat for a while with his fox's brush of a tail fanned out on the smooth planks. Behind Chang's back it was very bright and hot from the low rays of the sun. It must have been equally hot in Arabia, which was sliding by on the starboard side with its golden shore and black-brown hills, its peaks, also sprinkled with thick gold dust, looming like the mountains of a dead planet, and all its sandy, hilly wastes so incredibly clear that you felt as if you could easily jump across to them. High above on the bridge there was still a feeling of morning, cooled by a soft little current of air, and the mate – the same man who was later to drive Chang to distraction by blowing into his nostrils – strode up and down energetically, dressed all in white, in a white helmet and frightening dark glasses, glancing continuously skyward at the high spike of the foremast, above which a delicate wisp of cloud curled like an ostrich plume . . . Then from inside the Captain yelled: 'Chang, breakfast!', and jumping up Chang raced round the chart-house and hopped nimbly over its brass threshold. And there, over that threshold, it was even more pleasant than on the bridge: a wide brown leather couch was fixed to the wall, and an object glittering with glass and pointers resembling a round wall-clock hung above it, while standing on the floor was a slop basin filled with a mess of sweet milk and bread. Chang began to lap greedily, while the Captain busied himself with his duties: unrolling a large chart on a stand below the window opposite the couch, he placed a ruler upon it, and in crimson ink drew a long firm line. Chang finished his breakfast, and with drops of milk clinging to his whiskers jumped up onto the stand and sat down against the window, which was filled with a large expanse of navy blue collar and the broad back of the seaman standing at the spiked wheel. At this point the Captain who, as it later turned out, was very fond of a quiet chat when he and Chang were alone together, said:

'There you are, old fellow, there's the Red Sea for you. We'll have to find the most sensible way of getting across – just look at the pattern of all those little islands and reefs. I have to get you back to Odessa safe and sound because they already know about you there. I've already given the game away to a certain exceedingly capricious little girl, I've boasted about your charms, you see, on that line which those clever swine have laid at the bottom of every ocean . . . You know, Chang, I'm a terribly happy man, you can't imagine how happy, so naturally I'm terribly anxious not to hit one of those reefs and make a total fool of myself on my maiden voyage to distant parts.'

And while he was talking thus, the Captain suddenly glanced at Chang disapprovingly and boxed his ears.

'Paws off the chart!' he bellowed in the voice of command. 'Don't you dare climb over state property!'

Chang shook his head and growled, screwing up his eyes. This was the first blow he had ever received, his feelings were hurt and again it suddenly seemed to him that to live on this planet and to sail its seas was foul. He turned his head away, narrowed his eyes and, dimming their bright transparent light, growled softly and bared his fangs. But the captain appeared not to notice that Chang was upset. He lit a cigarette, returned to the couch, removed a gold watch from the side-pocket of his piqué monkey-jacket and, prising its lid open with one strong thumb-nail in order to gaze at something glittering and incredibly lively that was scampering noisily around inside, again began to speak in a friendly way. He again told Chang that he was taking him to Odessa, to Yelizavetinskaya Street where he, the Captain, had, first an apartment, secondly a beautiful wife, and thirdly an enchanting little daughter, and also that he, the Captain, was in spite of all a very happy man.

'A happy man in spite of all, Chang!' he said, and continued: 'That daughter, Chang, is a mischievous, inquisitive, obstinate little girl – things won't be easy at times, especially for your tail! But if you only knew, Chang, what an adorable creature she is! I love her so much, old fellow, that I'm even afraid of my love: she's the whole world to me, or let's say near enough the whole world – and can that be right? Yes, are we in general meant to love anyone so much?', he asked. 'Do you think all those Buddhas were any more stupid than you or me, and yet just listen to what they have to say about loving the world and all material things – no matter whether it's sunlight or waves or air, or a woman, or a child, or the scent of white acacia! And do you know about

Taoism, which is one of your own Chinese inventions? I don't know much about it myself, old fellow, and there doesn't seem to be anyone who knows very much more, but as far as I can gather, it's like this. There is a Great Mother of the Abyss who gives birth and then devours, and when she's devoured, again gives birth to all creation – in other words that is The Way of all creation, against which no creature on earth should rebel. But we rebel at every turn, at every turn try to alter not only, shall we say, the soul of a woman we love but the entire universe to suit ourselves. Life is frightening on this planet, Chang,' said the Captain, 'very sweet, but frightening – especially for people like me. I'm so very greedy for happiness and so often I come to grief. Is The Way dark and cruel, or is it exactly the opposite?'

And then, after a short pause, he added:

'Shall I tell you the point of all this? *When you love someone no power on earth can make you believe that you may not be loved in return.* And that, Chang, is where the trouble lies. But, my God, how wonderful life is, how wonderful!'

Tirelessly, blazing like a furnace beneath the sun which was already high in the heavens, the ship with an almost imperceptible shudder sliced its way through the Red Sea, which lay suspended and becalmed in fathomless, shimmering, transparent space. The shining empty face of the tropical sky gazed in through the door of the chart-house. It was nearly mid-day and the brass threshold was on fire from the sun. The crystal waves rolled more and more slowly as they slid by the side, exploding with a blinding incandescence which enveloped the chart-house. Chang sat on the couch and listened to the Captain. The Captain, who had been patting him on the head, suddenly pushed him off onto the floor. 'No, old fellow, it's too hot!' But this time Chang wasn't offended: it was too good to be alive, that joyous noon. Later . . .

Here once again Chang's dream is interrupted.

'Come on, Chang!' the Captain says, swinging his legs down from the bed. And again, Chang finds to his surprise that he's not

on board a ship in the middle of the Red Sea, but in an attic in
Odessa, and that although it is indeed mid-day out there in the
streets, the hour, far from being joyous, is dark, depressing and
hostile. And he growls a little at the Captain for having disturbed
him. But the Captain, without paying any attention to him, puts
on an old uniform cap and overcoat and, hands deep in pockets
and back hunched, goes towards the door. Whether he likes it or
not, Chang is forced to jump down from the bed. The Captain
descends the staircase wearily and reluctantly, as if under some
tedious obligation. Chang tumbles down quite fast, stimulated by
the remains of that nervous irritation which inevitably arrives on
the heels of the bliss that vodka brings . . .

Yes, for two years now Chang and the Captain have been
whiling away the hours, day in day out, wandering from one
restaurant to the next: there they sit, drinking and nibbling, in
contemplation of the other drunks who are drinking and nibbling
beside them, amid the din, tobacco smoke and general stench . . .
Chang lies on the floor at the Captain's feet, while the Captain sits
smoking, his elbows anchored firmly on the table nautical
fashion, waiting for the time when in obedience to some self-
imposed law he must migrate to yet another café or restaurant:
Chang and the captain take breakfast in one place, coffee in
another, lunch in a third, and supper in a fourth. Usually the
Captain remains silent. But every so often he'll bump into one of
his old cronies from the past and spend the entire day talking
about the futility of life, pouring out endless glasses of wine for
himself, for his interlocutor and for Chang who always has some
little dish on the floor beside him. And that is precisely how this
particular day will be spent: they have arranged to meet one of
the Captain's old friends, an artist in a silk hat, for lunch. That
means that to begin with they'll sit in a stinking beer parlour
surrounded by red-faced Germans – dull, business-like folk who
work from morning to night in order, it goes without saying, that
they may drink, eat, work again and engender their own kind;

then they'll progress to a café crammed to the rafters with Greeks and Jews who also lead a totally senseless, but in their case painfully agitated existence, dominated by a never-ending wait for stock exchange rumours; then they'll leave the café for the restaurant where all the dregs of humanity are assembled, and there they'll stay until the early hours of the morning . . .

The winter day is short, and with a bottle of wine in front of you and a friend to confide in it becomes shorter still. Thus Chang, the Captain and the artist, having already visited the beer parlour and the café, are now established drinking round after round in the restaurant. And again, elbows on the table, the Captain is fervently assuring the artist that there is only one truth in the world – a truth which is cruel and loathsome. 'Just look around you', he says, 'and consider all those people we meet day after day in the beer parlour, the café or the street. My friend, I've travelled the world over – life is the same everywhere you go. All those things people are supposed to live by are nothing but lies and rubbish: they have no God, no conscience, no rational goals in life, no love, no friendship, no honesty – there isn't even simple pity. Life is a dismal winter day in a filthy tavern, that's all . . .'

And lying under the table, Chang listens to this through a fog of alcohol in which there is no longer even a spark of animation. Does he agree with the Captain or not? We can't say for certain, and that being the case, things must be bad. Whether the Captain is right or wrong, Chang neither knows nor understands; and yet it is only when we are sad that we all say: 'I don't know. I don't understand', for in moments of joy every living creature is convinced that it knows and understands everything . . . But suddenly a ray of sunshine seems to pierce the fog, there's the sound of a baton tapping against the music-stand on the res-taurant's stage and first one, then two, then finally three violins begin to sing . . . Their song swells with ever-increasing passion, and in a trice Chang's soul becomes flooded with a different kind of anguish and melancholy. It trembles with incomprehensible rapture, with a kind of sweet torment and a thirsting for something, and Chang no longer knows whether he is awake or dreaming. He surrenders his whole being to the music, following it submissively into another world, and once again sees himself on the threshold of that beautiful place, a foolish trusting puppy on the deck of a ship in the middle of the Red Sea.

'Yes, and then what happened?', he asks himself in his dream, or his half-awake thoughts. 'Oh yes, I remember: it was good to be alive in the noon-time heat of that day in the Red Sea.' For a while Chang and the Captain sat in the chart-house and then went out and stood on the bridge . . . Oh, how dazzling was the light and sparkle, the indigo blue and azure! How extraordinarily riotous the whites, reds and yellows of the sailors' shirts draped on the prow of the ship, their sleeves stiff and square against the sky! Then later, Chang together with the Captain and several other mariners, all with brick-red faces, glistening eyes and white foreheads beaded with sweat, sat down to lunch in the first-class passenger lounge beneath the buzz of an electric fan whirring in the corner, and afterwards had a little nap followed by tea and then supper, finally returning to the bridge next to the chart-house, where the steward had placed the Captain's deck-chair, gazing far beyond the sea to the sunset which gleamed, gently green and luminous, among the many-hued, many-shaped little clouds and the wine-red sun which, having already lost its rays, suddenly brushed against the misty horizon and elongated itself into the shape of a fiery mitre . . . The ship raced along after it amid the smooth hummocks of water, shot with the colours of blue and purple shagreen, which appeared to be flashing past her sides, but the sun hurried on and on – the sea seemed to be dragging it into itself – and grew smaller and smaller until all that was left of it was a long burning ember which trembled and was snuffed out, and no sooner was its light extinguished than the shadow of some indefinable melancholy seemed to fall upon the whole world, and the breeze, which had been gathering its strength as night approached, grew more restless. Staring into the dark flame of the sunset, the Captain sat with his head bared, his hair ruffled by the breeze and an expression of proud, brooding sorrow on his face, and you could tell that *in spite of all* he was happy, and that it was not merely this ship, steaming along at his decree, which was in his power, but a whole world, because at that moment he held the whole world in his soul – and because there was already, even then, the smell of drink on his breath . . .

And so night fell, in all its terror and magnificence. It was black and agitated with an unruly wind, and flooded by so much brilliance from the hissing waves which dashed themselves against the ship that sometimes Chang, trotting behind the Captain as he strode rapidly and repeatedly up and down the deck, would jump squealing away from the side. Then the Captain lifted Chang into his arms again, and putting his cheek against his thudding heart – after all, it was beating just like the Captain's – carried him to the far end of the deck, to the quarter-deck, and stood there for a long time in the darkness, while Chang was bewitched by a sublime and fearful spectacle: from far below the tall, mammoth stern and the muted roar of the screw spilled a myriad white-hot darts which fell with a dry rustling sound, while enormous cerulean stars and compact balls of dark blue tore themselves free, to be immediately carried away on the snowy, sparkling path laid by the ship, exploding with a light which, as it died, left them smoking with mysterious pale-green phosphorescence deep inside the seething hummocks of water. From all directions, the wind came beating softly and strongly into Chang's muzzle, parting and cooling the thick fur on his chest, and as he pressed himself firmly and intimately against the Captain, he breathed the scent of something that reminded him of cold wax and inhaled the deep open belly of the sea, while the stern shuddered, plunging and lifting in the grip of some omnipotent, immensely free force, and he rocked and rocked, peering excitedly into this blind, dark, but endlessly teeming, dully mutinous Abyss. And from time to time, some particularly mischievous and massive wave, rushing noisily past the stern, would shine with an eerie glow upon the Captain's hands and silvery clothing.

That same night the Captain brought Chang to his cabin, which was big and cosy and illuminated by a lamp with a red silk shade. Standing in the dappled light thrown by this lamp onto the writing table beside the Captain's bunk were two photographs: one showed a pretty, cross-looking little girl with ringlets, sitting sulkily and defiantly in a deep armchair, and the other was an almost full-length portrait of a young woman holding a white lacy parasol over her shoulder and wearing a wide lacy hat and an elegant spring gown – graceful, slender, and as exquisitely melancholy as a Georgian princess. And the Captain said above the pounding of the black waves outside the open porthole:

'That woman won't love us, you and me, you know . . . *There are some female souls, old fellow, that languish eternally, lost in some strange, melancholy craving for love, and so are unable ever to love anyone.* There are such souls – and who's to judge them in all their heartlessness and dishonesty, their dreams of going on the stage, of having a car of their own, of picnics on board yachts, of some sportsman with his greasy plastered-down hair parted in the middle? Who can make them out? To each his own, Chang, and don't they also follow the most secret commands of Tao, like any one of the sea creatures roaming freely through the glinting black chain-mail of those waves?'

'Oh, oh!' said the Captain, as he sank down into a chair and, shaking his head, began to untie the lace of a white shoe. 'How I suffered, Chang, when I first sensed that she was no longer entirely mine – that night when she went to the yacht club ball alone for the first time, and came back in the early hours like a faded rose, pale with exhaustion and lingering excitement, and with eyes that were huge and dark and so far away from me! If you could only know, Chang, with what inimitable skill she tried to trick me, her simple surprise when she asked me: 'Oh, poor thing, aren't you asleep yet?' I was left speechless and, of course, she understood immediately and said nothing more, just gave me a quick glance and began to undress silently. I wanted to kill her, but calmly and coolly she said: 'Help me undo the back of my dress' – and I walked over to her obediently and, with trembling hands, began to unfasten all those little hooks and buttons. And then, when I saw her body in the opening of the dress and the space between her shoulder-blades and the little chemise which she'd pulled off her shoulders and tucked into the top of her stays, as soon as I smelled the perfume of her dark hair and, glancing into the illuminated pier-glass, caught sight of her breasts pushing up out of her corselet . . .'

And without completing his sentence, the Captain made a gesture with his hand.

He undressed and, lying down on his bunk, turned out the light, while Chang, turning round and round as he settled himself into the leather chair which stood by the writing table, saw streaks of white flashing and sputtering flame furrowing the black shroud of the sea, and lights winking evilly on the dark horizon from which, now and then, a living, terrifying wave would roll with the sound of thunder and, rearing up above the side of the ship, stare into the cabin like some enchanted serpent, suffused with the jewelled light of countless eyes the colour of emeralds and sapphires, while the ship, thrusting it aside, steamed evenly on through the heavy, undulating mass of this primeval, and for us alien and hostile essence we call the ocean . . .

During the night the Captain suddenly cried out, and startling himself by this cry which resounded with a kind of humiliatingly pitiful passion, immediately woke up. He lay there, silent for a moment, then sighed and said with a laugh: 'Yes, oh yes. "As a jewel of gold in a swine's snout – so is a fair woman." You are thrice right, Solomon the Wise.'

He found a cigarette box in the dark and lit a cigarette, but having taken one or two puffs, lowered his hand and fell asleep with a little red light glowing between his fingers. And again it became quiet – there was only the sound of the waves which streamed, sparkling and heaving, past the side. The Southern Cross appeared out of the black clouds . . .

But here Chang is deafened by a sudden clap of thunder and leaps to his feet in horror. What is it? Piloted by her inebriated captain, has the ship foundered on a submerged rock again, as she did three years ago? Has the Captain fired a pistol again at his beautiful, melancholy wife? No, he is not surrounded by night and sea, and he's not in Yelizavetinskaya Street on a winter afternoon, but in the blinding light of a noisy, smoky restaurant: it's the Captain striking the table with his fist and yelling drunkenly at the artist:

'Rubbish, rubbish! "As a jewel of gold in a swine's snout", that's woman for you! "I have decked my bed with coverings of tapestry, with fine linens of Egypt. Come let us take our fill of love until the morning, for the goodman is not home . . ." Aah-ah, woman! "Her house is the way to hell, going down to the chambers of death." But that's enough, enough, my friend. They're closing the place up – let's be off.'

And in a moment the Captain, Chang and the artist find themselves out in the dark street where the snow filled wind is blowing out the lanterns. The Captain kisses the artist and they go their separate ways. Chang, surly and half-asleep, trots sideways along the pavement behind the fast-retreating, swaying figure of the Captain . . . Yet another day has passed – was it dream or reality? – and again the world is dark and cold and filled with exhaustion . . .

And so Chang's days and nights go slipping past, each one the same as the one before. Until suddenly one day the world crashes like a ship which has been driven at full-steam upon a reef lying hidden from inattentive eyes beneath the sea. Waking one wintry morning, Chang is amazed at the deep silence which reigns in the room. He jumps up, races to the Captain's bed, and sees that he is lying with his head thrown back, his face white and still, and the eyelashes on his half-open lids motionless. And at the sight of those lashes, Chang gives a howl of agony and despair, as if a car, hurtling along the boulevard, had hurled him to the ground and cut him in two.

Then later, when the door stands wide-open and crowds of people come and go and come again, talking in loud voices – caretakers, policemen, the artist in the silk hat and all those others with whom the Captain used to sit around in restaurants – Chang seems to be turning to stone. Oh, how frightening were the things he had heard the Captain say: 'In the days when the keepers of the house shall tremble . . . and those that look out of their windows be darkened . . . when they shall be afraid of that which is high and fears shall be in the way . . . because man goeth to his long home and the mourners go about the streets . . . and the pitcher is broken at the fountain and the wheel broken at the cistern . . .' But now Chang no longer feels even horror. He lies on the floor, his muzzle turned towards the corner and his eyes shut tight, so as not to see the world, so as to forget it exists. And the world roars dully and distantly over him, like the sea over the head of someone sinking deeper and deeper into its abyss.

When he comes to again, he finds that he is already on a porch close to the doors of a church. He sits by them, dazed, his head hanging down, scarcely alive save for a slight tremor in his whole body. Then, suddenly, the church doors are flung open and Chang's eyes and heart are overwhelmed by an achingly beautiful, reverberating sight: in front of him lies a shadowy Gothic hall studded with stars of red light and decked in forests of tropical vegetation, with an oak coffin raised high upon a black dais, a dark mass of people and two women who in the perfect marble beauty of their deep mourning are like an elder and younger sister – and the air above is filled with a rumble and a thunder, the

discordant lamentations of priests loudly celebrating the sorrow-
ful joy of angels, a triumphant commotion and grandeur, while
flooding over everything comes the sound of unearthly canticles.
And in the face of this clamorous vision, all Chang's hackles rise
in pain and joy. The artist, stepping out of the church at this
moment, his eyes red from weeping, stops in amazement.

'Chang!' he says anxiously, bending over him. 'Chang, what is it?'
He touches Chang's head with a trembling hand, bends down
further still, and their eyes meet brimming with tears and such
love for one another that, silently, all of Chang's being cries out to
the world: 'No, oh no, there's another truth on earth, one I can't
see, a third truth!'

That day, returning from the cemetery, Chang moves in with
his third master – again high up in an attic, but this one warm and
scented with cigar-smoke, strewn with carpets and filled with
antique furniture, enormous paintings and brocade hangings . . .
The light is fading, the fireplace is glowing with a smouldering
dark crimson heat, and Chang's new master sits in an armchair.
When he came home he didn't even bother to remove his coat and
silk hat and he now sits smoking a cigar in his deep chair, staring
into the twilight of his studio . . . And Chang rests, stretched out
on a carpet in front of the fire, his eyes closed and his muzzle on
his front paws.

Someone else is also resting now – across the darkening city
behind the paling of the cemetery, in what we call a vault or
tomb. But that someone isn't the Captain. For if Chang loves the
Captain, and feels his presence, and sees him through the eyes of
memory, that God-given sight which none of us can understand,
then the Captain is still with him; in that world which has no begin-
ning and no end and is beyond the reach of Death. In that world
there can be only one truth – the third – but what it is is known
only to the final Master to whom Chang too must soon return.

Vasilyevskoye, 1916

Temir-Aksak-Khan

Translated by Sophie Lund

'Ah-ah-ah, Temir-Aksak-Khan!' From a coffee-house deep in the Crimean countryside comes the wild howl of a voice pulsating with hopeless, passionate anguish.

The spring night is dark and damp, the black wall of the mountainous precipices hardly discernible. An open motor-car stands on the white mud of the metalled road close to where the coffee-house is clinging to the rock-face, and two long, horizontal, incandescent pillars of smoke stretch from its fearsome, blinding orbs into the darkness ahead. From far below comes the sound of the invisible sea, and a moist restless breeze blows out of the gloom on every side.

The coffee-house is filled with smoke, dimly lit by a little iron lantern hanging from the ceiling, and heated by a pile of red-hot embers glowing on a hearth in the corner. The beggar who has launched straight into his song about Temir-Aksak-Khan with that excruciating cry sits on the clay floor. He is a hundred-year-old monkey in a sheepskin coat and a shaggy astrakhan cap rusted by rain, sun and time. On his knees he holds something that resembles a crude wooden lyre. He is leaning forward, and as his face is hidden, his audience can see only the brown ears protruding from under his cap. From time to time tearing harsh sounds out of his strings, he howls with unbearable, despairing sorrow.

On a stool close to the hearth sits the effeminately plump, pleasant-looking Tartar who is the proprietor of the coffee-house. At first his smile seems to denote affection mixed with just a little sadness, or perhaps a patronizing irony. Then he becomes transfixed, his eyebrows raised, the smile frozen into one of pain and bewilderment.

Sitting on a bench under the little window, a tall Hadji with thin shoulder-blades and a grey beard has been smoking quietly; he is dressed in a black robe and a white turban which sets off to perfection the swarthy darkness of his features. Now he has forgotten his pipe, tipped his head back against the wall, and closed his eyes. One leg, clad in a striped stocking, is bent at the knee and rests on the bench, the other dangles loose in its slipper.

And at a little table near the Hadji sit the travellers who have taken it into their heads to stop their automobile and venture into this rustic coffee-house for a cup of atrocious coffee: a portly gentleman wearing a bowler hat and an English mackintosh, and a beautiful young woman whose face is pale with concentration and emotion. She comes from the south and knowing the language of the Tartars can understand the words of the song, 'Ah-ah-ah, Temir-Aksak-Khan!'

There was no khan in the universe more glorious than Temir-Aksak-Khan. All the world that lay beneath the moon trembled before him, and the fairest women and maidens on earth were ready to lay down their lives for a single moment of joy as his slave. Yet before he died Temir-Aksak-Khan sat in the dust and on the stones of the market-place and kissed the rags covering the beggars and cripples that passed his way, and cried out to them:

'Pluck out my soul, o ye beggars and cripples. For even the desire for desire has forsaken it.'

And when the Lord at last took pity on him and delivered him from the earth's empty glory and the earth's empty pleasures, all his kingdoms soon fell, his cities and palaces crumbled, and the sands drifted like ashes over their ruins beneath the eternal, precious blue glaze of the sky and the eternal flames of the sun that burned like the fires of hell. *Ah-ah-ah, Temir-Aksak-Khan! Where are your days and your deeds? Where are your battles and victories? Where are those young tender jealous ones that loved you, where are the eyes that blazed like black suns on your couch?*

Everyone is silent, under the spell of the song. But it is strange: that desperate sorrow and that bitter reproach with which it throbs are sweeter than the most sublime, most passionate joy.

The gentleman traveller stares fixedly down at the table, puffing furiously at his glowing cigar. His companion has opened her eyes wide and tears are rolling down her cheeks.

Dazed, they remain seated for a while and then go out onto the porch of the coffee-house. The beggar, having ended his song, begins to chew and tear pieces off the unleavened loaf that the proprietor has brought him. Yet it seems as if the song is still lingering on, that it has and forever will have no end.

As she was leaving, the young woman handed the beggar a whole gold piece, but now wonders anxiously whether it was enough and wishes she could return to give him another one – or rather another two or three, or perhaps, in front of everyone, kiss his leathery hand. Tears are still burning her eyes, but she feels she has never been happier than at this moment, after the song about all being vanity and sorrow beneath the sun has faded, and on this dark, damp night with the distant murmur of the invisible sea, the scent of spring rain and the restless breeze which reaches deep into her very soul.

The chauffeur, who has been lounging in his vehicle, hastily jumps out, bends down in the glare of the head-lights to attend to something, like some furry animal in his coat which appears to be inside-out, and the engine suddenly bursts into life, roaring and shuddering in its impatience. After helping the young woman into the car, the gentleman sits down beside her and covers her knees with a rug, and, absent-mindedly, she thanks him. The motor-car races down the even slope of road, shoots up a rise, leaning its bright pillars against some bush or other, and then again swings them to the side, dropping them into the darkness of a new descent . . . High above the outline of the scarcely visible

mountains which loom like giants, stars sparkle among the
insubstantial clouds, and far ahead in the distance is the faint
white blur of the breakers lining the curve of the bay, and the
breeze blows soft and strong in their faces . . .

Oh, Temir-Aksak-Khan, said the song, there was none more
valiant or fortunate or glorious than you beneath the moon, dark
of face, fiery of gaze – radiant and bountiful as Gabriel, wise and
magnificent as King Suleiman! Brighter and greener than the
leaves of Paradise was the silk of your turban, trembling and
shimmering with the seven-hued brilliance of stars was the
diamond plume upon it, and all the fairest princesses and
slave-girls on earth were ready to die for the joy of touching their
lips to your dark narrow hand, decked in all the rings of the
Indies. Yet when you had drained the cup of earthly pleasures, you
sat in the dust of the market-place, Temir-Aksak-Khan, and caught
and kissed the rags covering the cripples that passed your way:

'Pluck out my suffering soul, o ye cripples!'

And the centuries have flown past above your forgotten grave,
and the sands have closed over the ruins of your mosques and
palaces beneath the eternally blue sky and the unpitying, joyous
sun, and the wild rose has crept through the fragments of azure
faience on your tomb, so that with each new spring nightingales
may return again and again to grieve upon it, their hearts
breaking with the sweet agony of their song and the unutterable
joy of their sorrow . . . *Ah-ah-ah, Temir-Aksak-Khan, where is your
bitter wisdom now? Where are all the torments of your soul, the tears and
the gall that swept away the honeyed delusions of this world?*

The mountains have stepped back, and already the sea is racing
along beside the highway, surging with a hiss and the smell of
crabs onto the white shingle of the shore. Far ahead in the dark
lowlands there is a scattering of red and white lights and the rosy
aureole of a town, while the night that stretches above it and
above the bay is black and soft as soot.

Paris, 1921

Long Ago

Translated by Sophie Lund

Once upon a time, a thousand years ago, there lived with me on the Arbat, in a hotel called The North Pole, a certain Ivan Ivanych, unheard, unnoticed, the humblest man in all the world, already quite elderly and bedraggled.

Year after year, Moscow went on with its life, tackling its enormous tasks. He also tackled something, and had some reason for existing on this planet. At about nine o'clock he'd go out, and return at about five. Thinking quiet but not at all despondent thoughts, he'd take his key off its hook in the porter's lodge, ascend to the second floor and walk along the L-shaped corridor. In the corridor there was a complex smell of something very unpleasant, especially of whatever it is, pungent and suffocating, that is used to polish the floors of cheap hotels. The corridor was dark and sinister (the windows of the rooms looked out on to a central well, and the glass panes above their doors gave little light), and all day a small lamp with a reflector burned at the far end of each of its stretches. However, Ivan Ivanych appeared not to experience even the tiniest particle of those mournful feelings which that corridor roused in people who weren't used to The North Pole. He would walk calmly and simply along the corridor. Fellow residents would pass him: a student with bright eyes and a youthful beard hurrying eagerly along struggling into the sleeves of his tunic; a typist with an independent air, strapping and seductive, in spite of her resemblance to a white-skinned negress; a little brown-haired old lady in high heels, unfailingly rouged and resplendent, with a constant liquid gurgle

in her chest, her appearance always preceded by the swift
murmur along the corridor of tiny bells attached to her snub-
nosed pug, with its protruberant lower jaw and savage, senseless-
ly bulging eyes . . . Ivan Ivanych bowed politely to everyone he
met, and bore not the slightest grudge when there was hardly so
much as a nod in reply. He would trudge along one arm of an L,
turn into an even longer and darker one, where the rosy sparkle of
the little wall-light was even further ahead, thrust a key into his
door – and disappear behind it until the following morning.

What did he do in his lodgings, how did he while away his
hours? God knows. His domestic existence, which didn't reveal
itself by any outward signs, was of no use to anyone and a
mystery to everyone – even to the chamber-maid and floor waiter
who broke into his seclusion only to bring a samovar, or make the
bed, or clean the vile wash basin from which a jet of water
spurted, always unexpectedly, always away from your hands and
face, directed high, sideways, or at an angle. A life of rare
obscurity, I repeat, rare uniformity, was that of Ivan Ivanych.
Winter would pass, spring come. Trams raced, thundering and
jingling, along the Arbat, a ceaseless flow of pedestrians hurried
towards each other on their way to unknown destinations, cabs
rattled by, street hawkers yelled, carrying trays upon their heads,
towards evening in the distant gap above the street the sky shone
with a luminous golden sunset, and melodiously flooding over all
these sounds and noises, the bass voice of bells rang out from an
ancient octagonal belltower. Ivan Ivanych seemed not to hear or
see any of this . . . Neither winter nor spring, summer nor
autumn had any visible effect upon him or his way of life. Until,
one spring day, a certain prince arrived from somewhere, took a
room at The North Pole, and became Ivan Ivanych's closest
neighbour. Ivan Ivanych succumbed to something completely
unforeseen and unsuspected.

What was it about the prince that so amazed him? Obviously
not the title – after all, there was that ancient fellow resident, the

little lady with the pug, also a person of title, for whom he felt absolutely nothing. What did the prince possess that was so captivating? Obviously not wealth or appearance – he had been a great spendthrift and was extremely seedy in appearance, being enormous, ill-proportioned, with bags under his eyes and noisily, painfully short of breath. Yet Ivan Ivanych was amazed and captivated and, above all, completely driven off his long-established course. His existence was transformed into a kind of constant ferment. He plunged himself into a frenzy of agitated, petty, shameful imitation.

The prince arrived, moved in, began to come and go, see people, busy himself with this and that – in exactly the same way, naturally, as all those others who had stayed at The North Pole within Ivan Ivanych's memory, a vast number whose friendship it had never entered his head to seek. But the prince he singled out, for some reason, from all the rest. For some reason, face to face with the prince upon the second or third occasion they met in the corridor, he clicked his heels, presented himself, and offering all manner of profuse apologies, inquired what, as near as possible, was the correct time. And having struck up an acquaintance in this adroit fashion, he simply fell in love with the prince, which threw the usual pattern of his days into total disarray, and began to follow slavishly in virtually the prince's every footstep.

The prince, for example, went to bed late. He would return home at two a.m. (always by cab). Ivan Ivanych's lamp also began to burn until two. He would wait up, Heaven knows why, for the prince's return, for his heavy tread in the corridor, his whistling breath. He waited with joy, almost with trepidation, and sometimes would even peer out of his little room to see the approaching prince and to exchange a few words with him. The prince would advance unhurriedly, as if he hadn't noticed, and in a profoundly indifferent tone of voice, always ask one and the same question:

'Ah, so you're not in bed yet?'

And Ivan Ivanych, breathless with rapture, although, it must be said, without a trace of diffidence or servility, would reply:

'No, Prince, I'm not in bed yet. The night's still young, it's only ten past two . . . You've been out enjoying yourself?'

'Yes,' the prince would say, wheezing and making vain attempts to get his key into the key-hole. 'I met an old friend, we stopped off for a drink . . . Goodnight.'

Upon this things would end, with the prince coldly yet politely cutting short his nocturnal chat with Ivan Ivanych, but for Ivan Ivanych even this was enough. On tip-toe he would return to his room, automatically perform the customary procedures before retiring, cross himself a couple of times while bowing to the corner of the room, climb silently into bed behind the partition, and fall asleep immediately, utterly happy and utterly devoid of self-interest, even in the very remotest of any intentions he might have had towards the prince, unless one were to count those most innocent lies he used to tell the floor waiter in the morning:

'Well, I was up late again last night . . . The prince and I sat up talking, again, till dawn . . .'

When evening came, the prince would place his large battered shoes outside the door and hang out his vast silver-coloured trousers. Ivan Ivanych, too, began to put out his small wrinkled boots, which in the past had been cleaned on each of the twelve Holy Festivals, and hang out his little breeches with torn-off buttons which had previously never emerged at all, not even at Christmas or Easter.

The prince always woke early, coughing dreadfully, greedily lit a plump cigarette, opened his door into the corridor, shouted for the whole house to hear: 'Waiter! Tea!' – and in a dressing-gown and flapping slippers, disappeared for a long time upon a matter of necessity. Ivan Ivanych began to do the same – he too yelled into the corridor for the samovar and, with galoshes on his bare feet and a little summer overcoat over his faded underclothes, also hurried off, although previously he'd always gone in the evening.

One day the prince mentioned that he was very fond of the circus and often went there. Ivan Ivanych, who had never liked circuses and hadn't visited one for at least forty years, resolved to go too, and having done so, rapturously informed the prince that same night of the enormous pleasure it had given him.

Oh, the spring, the spring! The whole business can best be explained by the fact that this nonsense took place in spring.

Each spring is like the end of something that has at last worn out, and the beginning of something new. During that long-ago Moscow spring this deception was especially strong and sweet – for me because I was young and my student days were nearly over, for many others because it was a spring of rare beauty. Every spring is a festival, and that spring was particularly festive.

Moscow had lived through its difficult, exhausting winter. Then it had lived through Lent and Easter, and again felt as if it had finished something, lifted a burden from its shoulders, survived the wait for something real. And there were countless Muscovites already changing or preparing to change their lives, preparing to start life again, as it were, from the beginning, and this time to live in a different way, not as before, but more sensibly, properly, youthfully, hastening to clean their apartments, order summer outfits, visit the shops – and shopping (even for mothballs) is fun! – preparing themselves, in a word, for the exodus from Moscow, for restful times at dachas, or in the Caucasus, the Crimea, abroad, for summer in general, which is bound, it always seems, to be happy and long, so long . . .

How many splendid suitcases and new creaking baskets, filling the soul with joy, were purchased at that time in Leontev Lane and from Muir & Merrilees! How many people were shorn and barbered at Basil's or Theodore's! And one after the other came sunlit, exciting days, days filled with new scents, a new cleanliness in the streets, a new sparkle to the church cupolas against the brilliant sky, with a new Strastnoy Street, a new Petrovka, the bright new attire of belles and beauties flying past in elegant light-weight carriages along Kuznetsky Avenue, with the new pale-grey hat of some famous actor also flying past upon soft rubber tyres on his way somewhere. Everyone seemed to have rounded off a column in their previous unsatisfactory existence, and practically all of Moscow was on the eve of a new life which couldn't fail to bring happiness – I was too, especially so, much more than anyone else, it appeared to me at the time. Closer and closer came the day of my parting from The North Pole, from everything which had been my student life there, and from morning to night I was immersed in activity, in journeys across Moscow, in a variety of joyous preoccupations. And what was my next-door hotel neighbour, that most humble of all our contemporaries, doing at the time? Why, much the same as all of us. When all was said and done, he was going through the same experience as the rest.

It was April, then May, trams raced jingling by, a ceaseless flow of pedestrians hurried along, cabs rattled past, sadly and tenderly – although the matter in hand was merely asparagus– street hawkers cried their wares carrying trays upon their heads, a sweet aroma floated from Skachkov's cake shop, bay trees stood in tubs at the entrance of The Prague, where fine folk were already partaking of new potatoes and sour cream, day melted imperceptibly into evening, and already a luminous golden sunset shone in the sky to the west, while melodiously flooding over this crowded happy street, the bass voice of bells rang out from an ancient octagonal belltower . . . Day after day, the spring city lived its gigantic varied existence, and I was among the happiest of those who took part, drinking in all its scents, sounds, commotions, encounters, trading and buying, as I hailed cabs, dropped into Tremblay's Café with friends, ordered fish soup at The Prague, chased down cold glasses of vodka with bites of fresh cucumber . . . And Ivan Ivanych? Well, Ivan Ivanych also went

off somewhere, did something of his own, some small, terribly
small, thing, which procured him the right to the tiniest existence
among us – to a thirty-kopek dinner at the eating-house opposite
The North Pole, and to a room at The North Pole itself. This
modest right was the only thing he had managed to earn for
himself, wherever it was he went, to do whatever it was he did,
and you would have thought him a total stranger to all our hopes
for a new life, for a new coat and trousers, a new hat, a new
haircut, for some means of measuring up to some other person,
for striking up an acquaintance, a friendship . . . But then the
prince arrived.

What was it about him that so enchanted and astonished Ivan
Ivanych? But then, it isn't the object of enchantment that counts,
but our thirst for enchantment itself. Besides, the prince was a
man who still retained vestiges of the grand manner, a man who
had thoroughly squandered his life, but who, it follows, must in
his day have known how to live. And so poor Ivan Ivanych began
yearning for a new spring-time existence too, one containing a
little mild ostentation and even a few distractions. Well, is that so
wrong – not to tumble into bed at ten o'clock, to hang out your
trousers for pressing, to answer nature's call before washing in
the morning? Doesn't it make you seem younger to pop in for a
haircut, to have your beard trimmed and shortened, to buy a grey
boyish little hat, and to return home with some small purchase,
even if it's only a quarter of a pound of trifles prettily wrapped by
the hands of some charming lady assistant? And Ivan Ivanych,
gradually falling deeper and deeper into temptation, went
through it all in his own way, in other words accomplished, as far
as his strength and circumstances allowed, all that was accom-
plished by others: he struck up new friendships, and postured
(admittedly, no worse than anyone else!) and acquired some
spring clothes, and gathered a few spring-time hopes, and
brought a measure of spring-time dissipation into his life, and
learned extravagant habits, and trimmed his beard, and began

returning to The North Pole in the early evening clutching small packages of some sort; and going even further, invested in a little grey hat and an item of luggage – a modest one rouble seventy-five kopek suitcase covered in shiny tin studs – dreaming of going that summer without fail to the Holy Trinity or the New Jerusalem Monastery . . .

Whether this dream came true, and what, in fact, happened to Ivan Ivanych's impulse towards a new existence, I really don't know. I have an idea that, as with most of our impulses, nothing much came of it, but I repeat, I cannot say for sure. And the reason why I cannot is that very soon all of us, that is the prince, Ivan Ivanych and I, parted, and parted one fine day, not for the summer, not for a year, not for two years, but for all eternity. Yes, for nothing short of eternity – never, at any moment until the end of the world, to meet again, a thought which now, for all its apparent oddity, I find simply terrifying: just think – never! All of us living at a certain time on this planet together, and together experiencing all its earthly joys and sorrows, seeing the same sky, loving and hating what are, after all, the same things, each and every one of us condemned to suffer the same sentence, the same disappearance off the face of the earth, should really nurture the greatest tenderness towards each other, a feeling of the most heart-rending closeness, and should be literally scream-ing with terror and pain whenever we are parted by a fate which at any moment is fully capable of transforming every one of our separations, even if only meant to last ten minutes, into an eternal one. But as you know, for most of the time, we are a long way from such sentiments, and often take leave of even those closest to us in the most thoughtless manner imaginable. That, of course, is how we parted – the prince, Ivan Ivanych and I. A cab was fetched early one evening to take the prince to the Smolensk railway station, a drab little vehicle for sixty kopeks, and another one costing a silver rouble and a half, harnessed to a frisky grey mare, to take me to the Kursk station – and we parted without even saying goodbye to each other. So Ivan Ivanych was left behind in his dark gloomy corridor, in his cage with dim glass above the door, while the prince and I drove off in completely opposite directions, shoving tips into every hand and settling into our separate cabs – the prince, I believe, fairly indifferent, and I buoyant, dressed from head to toe in brand-new clothes, vaguely anticipating some marvellous encounter in the railway carriage, on the journey . . . And I remember as if it were now: I drove towards the Kremlin, a Kremlin lit by the evening sun, went through the Kremlin and past its cathedrals – oh, my God, how beautiful they were! – then along the Ilinka, redolent of paints and oils and already bathed in evening shadow, and along Pokrovka, already lying beneath the protection of booming, clamouring bells, ringing a blessing upon the happy close of a busy day – I drove, not merely pleased with myself and the world at large, but truly engulfed in the ecstasy of being alive, and no sooner had we reached Arbat Square than I forgot, in a flash, about The North Pole, and the prince, and Ivan Ivanych, and would doubtless have been most surprised had someone told me then that they too would be preserved for ever in that sweet bitter dream of the past by which my soul will live until the grave, and that a day would come when I'd be calling out in vain to them too:

'Dear Prince, dear Ivan Ivanych, where are your bones rotting now? And where are those foolish hopes and joys we shared, where is our long-ago Moscow spring?'

Amboise, 1922

An Unknown Friend

Translated by Sophie Lund

7th October

On this post–card with its sad, majestic scene of a moonlit night by the shores of the Atlantic Ocean, I hasten to send you my warmest thanks for your latest book. These shores are my second home. Ireland. See how far this greeting from an unknown friend has come to find you! I wish you joy, and may God bless you.

8th October

Here's another view of this lonely land to which fate has driven me for the rest of time.

Yesterday, in a terrible downpour – it's always raining here – I went into town on various errands, and having happened to buy your book, read it without stopping the entire journey back to the villa where we live the whole year round for the sake of my health. It was almost dark from all the rain and clouds, the flowers and leaves in the gardens were incredibly bright, the empty tram sped along amid flashes of violet light, and I sat there reading on and on, feeling, somehow, an almost painful happiness.

Farewell, I thank you once again. There seems to be something more I should say to you. But what? I don't know and can't decide.

10th October

I can't resist the temptation to write to you again. I'm afraid you must receive far too many letters of this kind. And yet these letters are merely the echoes of those human hearts for whom your work is intended. So why should I stay silent? By releasing your book to the world, and so to me as well, it was you who made the first approach . . .

Today the rain has been falling again without cease on our unnaturally green garden, my room is dark and gloomy, and a fire has been burning in the grate since morning. There's so much that I should like to say to you, but you know better than most how difficult, how almost impossible it is to explain oneself. I'm still filled with a sense of something incomprehensible, insoluble, and yet so wonderful, for which I'm in your debt – can you tell me what it is, this feeling? And in general, what it is that human beings experience when they submit to the influence of art? Is it delight at man's skill and power? A heightening of that longing for personal happiness which is always, always, present within us, and which comes to life so vividly when we are exposed to anything that acts upon our emotions – music, poetry, some pictorial memory, a certain scent? Or could it be the joy of experiencing the divine beauty of the human soul when someone very rare, like you, reminds us that this divine beauty really does exist? Sometimes I'll be reading something – at times it might even be something horrifying – and all of a sudden I'll find myself saying: God, how beautiful this is! What can it mean? It means, perhaps – when all is said and done, how beautiful life is!

Goodbye, I'll write to you again soon. I feel sure that there can be nothing indelicate in my doing so, and that it is not improper to correspond with authors. And anyway, you can choose not to read my letters . . . although, of course, that would make me very sad.

Night

Forgive me, this may sound unfortunate, but I feel compelled to say it: I'm not young and have a fifteen-year-old daughter who's already a grown-up young lady, yet there was a time when I wasn't altogether unattractive and I haven't changed that much over the years . . . I just wouldn't wish you to imagine me other than I am.

11th October

I wrote to you impelled by the need to share the emotion aroused in me by your talent, which affected me like the sound of sad, sublime music. Why does it exist, this need for sharing? I have no idea and neither have you, yet we both know perfectly well that in some way it is burned into the human heart, that there's no life without it and that it contains a great mystery. After all, when you write your books you too are merely responding to this need, and what's more – you abandon your whole self to it completely.

I've always read a great deal – and kept many diaries, in common with all those whose lives are unfulfilled – and I still read widely, I've read your work before, but not very often, I mostly knew you by reputation. And now this latest book of yours . . . How strange! Somewhere, somehow, a hand puts pen to paper, a soul reveals a tiny particle of its secret existence by the tiniest possible hint – for what can words express, even words such as yours! – and suddenly there's no space, no time, no differences of fate or circumstance, and all your thoughts and feelings are mine, are both of ours. Truly, there is but one universal soul on earth. And doesn't that make my impulse to write to you understandable – to communicate my feelings and share something and complain a little? Aren't the works you create and the letters I write to you one and the same? For you too are trying to reach someone, to express some kind of feeling, when you send your lines through space towards some invisible person. You know, you too are complaining – more often than not, only complaining! – for our complaints are synonymous with that cry for understanding which is so fundamental to every human being: how often it occurs in songs and prayers, in poetry and the outpourings of love!

Perhaps you'll answer me, if only briefly? Please answer.

13th October

Again I write to you at night, from my bedroom where I'm plagued by an incomprehensible desire to say something which might easily sound naïve and which, in any case, won't come out the way it's meant. And in fact I have very little to say: only that I feel very sad and very sorry for myself – and that at the same time I'm made happy by my sadness and self-pity. It saddens me to think that I'm somewhere in a foreign country on the westernmost shores of Europe, in some kind of villa outside town, amid the darkness of this autumn night and the fog which comes rolling in from a sea stretching all the way to America. It's sad that I'm alone, not just in this charming, cosy room, but in the whole world. And saddest of all is that you, whom I've invented and from whom I now expect something, should be so terribly far away from me, so mysterious and, of course, whatever I may say, so alien and indeed, I fear, so right to be so . . .

When you consider it everything in the world is beautiful, even the lampshade on this lamp and the golden light it sheds, the gleaming linen on my turned-down bed and my dressing-gown, my foot in its slipper and my thin hand in its wide sleeve. And I feel an endless pity towards everything: what is it all for? Everything passes and everything will pass and everything is futile, like this eternal waiting which has become my substitute for life.

I beg you to write to me. Only two or three words, of course, just to tell me that you can hear me. Forgive my persistence.

15th October

This is our town and our church. That deserted craggy shore – my first post-card to you – is further to the north. But the town and the church and everything here is so gloomy, so black. The granite, the slate, the asphalt and the perpetual rain . . .

Do send me a brief reply. I quite understand that you can have no more than two or three words to say to me and, believe me, I won't be in the slightest bit offended. But please, please write!

21st October

Alas, there's no letter from you. And yet two weeks have gone by since I first wrote . . .

However, perhaps your publisher hasn't forwarded my letters to you yet? Or perhaps you've been distracted by too many pressing engagements and social events? I find this very sad, but still preferable to the idea that you've simply chosen to ignore my plea. Such a thought is very painful and wounding. You'll say that I have no right to claim your attention, and that consequently there can be no room for my pain and my wounded feelings. And yet are you sure that I have no right? Perhaps as a result of my having experienced certain feelings towards you a right has come to exist. For example, has there ever been a single Romeo who hasn't demanded that his love be requited even when his hopes are unfounded, or any Othello who's not been jealous by rights? They both say: since I love, how can I possibly not be loved in return, how can I possibly be betrayed? This is not merely a simple desire to be loved, but something far greater and more complex. The love I feel for something or someone becomes part of me, part of my being . . . But I can't explain it adequately to you, I only know that this is the way human beings have always reacted and always will . . .

Be that as it may, there's still no reply from you and I'm

writing to you again. I suddenly invented the idea that you were somehow close to me – although, again, was it only an idea? – and believing in my own invention I began, stubbornly, to write. And I already know that the more I write, the more urgent my need to write will become, because some sort of link between us will grow stronger all the time. I can't imagine you at all, I can't even visualize your physical appearance. So who is it that I'm writing to? Myself? It doesn't matter. After all, I too am you.

22nd October

Today the weather is beautiful, my heart is light, all the windows are open, and the sun and the warm air remind me of spring. This is a very strange land! In summer it's wet and cold, in winter and autumn it's wet and warm, but from time to time there'll be a day so exquisite that you can no longer tell whether it's winter or part of an Italian spring. Oh, Italy, Italy, and my eighteen-year-old self, my hopes, my trusting joy, my expectations on the threshold of a life which was still all before me, and all bathed in a sunlit haze, like the hills, the valleys and flower gardens around Vesuvius! Forgive me, I know that what I'm saying is far from new, but what does that matter to me?

Night

Could it be that you haven't written to me because you find me too abstract? If so I'll give you a few more details about my life. I've been married for sixteen years. My husband is French. I met him one winter on the French Riviera, married him in Rome, and after our honeymoon trip through Italy, we came to settle here forever. I have three children, a little boy and two girls. Do I love them? Yes I do, but my love is a little different from that of most mothers, who live their lives only through their families and children. While the children were little I spent all my days looking after them, sharing all their games and occupations, but now they no longer need me and I'm left with a great deal of free time which I devote to reading. My relatives are far away, our lives have drifted apart and we have so few interests left in common that we hardly ever correspond. Because of my husband's position, I'm often required to go out in society, to receive and return visits, and attend dinners and evening functions. Yet I have no friends, male or female. I'm not like the ladies here and I don't believe in friendship between men and women . . .

But enough about me. If you reply, tell me just a little about yourself. What are you like? Where do you live? Do you prefer Shakespeare or Shelley, Goethe or Dante, Balzac or Flaubert? Are you fond of music, and if so which kind? Are you tied by a bond that has become tedious or have you a bride with whom you share that tender and exquisite hour when the world is new and full of rapture and there are no memories to sadden and deceive with thoughts of some unknown, unfulfilled happiness?

                                                            1st November

Still no letter from you. What torture! Torture so great that at times I curse the day and the hour when I decided to write to you.

And worst of all, there's no escape. However much I may tell myself that there'll be no letter and that there's nothing to wait for, I still find myself waiting; who can guarantee to me that a letter won't arrive? Oh, if only I could know for sure that you'll never write. I'd be happy even with that. And yet, no, no – it's better to hope. I'm hoping, and waiting!

                                                            3rd November

No letter, and my torture drags on . . .

As a matter of fact, only the morning hours are painful, when I dress, unnaturally calm and unhurried but with hands cold with hidden anguish, go down to breakfast, and then watch over my daughter as she sits at her piano practice, learning her exercises with such touching concentration and with her back so straight, so exquisitely straight, that it could only belong to a fifteen-year old girl. At last, at mid-day, the post arrives. I rush for it, find nothing – and am almost calm again until the following morning . . .

Today is another beautiful day. The sun is low, clear and gentle. The garden is full of autumn flowers and bare black trees, and there's something delicate, pale blue, incredibly lovely in the valleys beyond their branches. In my heart there's a feeling of gratitude towards someone, for something. For what? After all, there's nothing now and nothing waiting in the future . . . And yet is that really so, can there really be nothing when this feeling of gratitude moves my heart?

And I also thank you, for having given me the opportunity of inventing you. You'll never know me and never meet me, but even in that I find much melancholy beauty. And maybe it's just as well that you don't write, that you haven't written a single word to me, and that I can't imagine you in the flesh. For how could I have said these things to you and sensed you the way I do now if I'd known you, if you'd sent me even as much as one reply? Inevitably you would have been different, just a tiny bit disappointing, and I wouldn't have felt so free to write to you . . .

It's getting colder but I haven't closed the window and can still see the haze of pale blue on the lowlands and hills beyond the garden. There's an unbearable beauty in that blue – unbearable because it seems to be insisting on some response from me. What? I don't know. We know nothing!

5th November

All this is like a diary, and yet not quite, because now I have a reader, if only an imaginary one . . .

What is it that induces you to write? Is it the desire to tell a story or is it the need to explain yourself, if only in parables? The latter, of course. Nine-tenths of all writers, even the most famous of them, are just story-tellers, and so, in essence, have nothing in common with anything that could justifiably be described as art. And what is art? The prayer, the music, and the song of the human soul . . . Oh, if only I could leave just a line or two behind me to say that I too have lived and loved and rejoiced, that I've known youth and spring and Italy . . . that there's a faraway land by the shores of the Atlantic Ocean where I still live and love and wait for something even now . . . that there are wild, poverty-stricken islands in the midst of that ocean, a wild, poverty-stricken existence led by people who are alien to the rest of the world, and whose origins and dark tongue and purpose in life are unknown, and forever will be . . .

But still, I'm waiting and waiting for a letter. Now it has become like an obsession, like a kind of spiritual sickness.

7th November

It's astonishing. Day after day goes by and there's still no letter. And just think: because it doesn't arrive and there's been no reply from a man I've never seen and never will see, no echo to this voice that I've sent out somewhere into the distance, into my dreams, I've a sense of terrible loneliness, a sense of the terrible emptiness of the world. Emptiness, emptiness!

The rain and fog and humdrum days have returned. And that's really a good thing – it's familiar and appropriate. It calms me.

Goodbye, and may God forgive you your cruelty. For yes, it is cruel.

8th November

Three o'clock and it's already quite dark from the fog and the rain. And we're expecting friends to tea at five.

They'll arrive in the rain in motor-cars, out of that dismal town which is darker than ever when it's raining, with its wet black asphalt and wet black roofs and the spire of its black granite church disappearing into all that rain and gloom . . .

I'm already dressed as if I'm about to go on stage. I await the moment when I'll have to start saying all the right things, become charming, vivacious and solicitous, and only a little pale, something which can easily be explained by this dreadful weather. And in my finery I seem to have become much younger, I'm ready to burst into tears at any minute, and I feel as if I'm my own daughter's elder sister. For I've been through something strange, something akin to being in love. With whom? Because of what?

Farewell, I'm no longer waiting for anything – I say this with total sincerity.

10th November

Farewell, my mysterious friend. I conclude these unanswered letters of mine the same way as I began – with an expression of gratitude. I thank you for not responding. It would have been worse had you done so. For what could you have said to me? How could we have cut short our correspondence without causing each other embarrassment? And what more could I have found to say to you, other than what I have already said? There's nothing left – I've said it all. Really, about any human life, there are only two or three lines to be written. Yes, only two or three lines.

With a curious feeling of having lost someone I'm left alone again with my house, the nearness of the foggy ocean and these

autumn and winter days. And again I return to my diary, a
strange compulsion, which like your need to write, only God can
understand.

Several days ago I saw you in a dream. You were somehow
strange, silent and invisible, sitting in a corner of a darkened
room. And yet I could see you. And even asleep I asked myself:
how is it possible in a dream to see someone you have never seen
in reality? God alone creates out of nothing. It made me very
uneasy and I awoke in fear and anguish.

It is very probable that in fifteen or twenty years time neither
you nor I will still be on this planet. To our meeting in the next
world! Who can be sure that it doesn't exist? After all, we can't
understand our own dreams, the products of our own imagina-
tion. Does it belong to us, that imagination, or more precisely,
what we call our imagination, our inventions and longings? Is it
in obedience to our own will that we yearn towards another soul
as I yearn towards yours?

Farewell. Or no, let it be Goodbye, until we meet again.

Alpes Maritimes, 1923

At Sea, At Night

Translated by Sophie Lund

During the night, the ship which was on its way from Odessa to the Crimea dropped anchor outside Eupatoria.

On board the vessel and around her all hell broke loose. There came the rumble of winches and the angry cries of those hauling the cargo on to the deck and those unloading it from an enormous barge below; the passenger gangplank crashed down amid sounds of fighting and yelling, and with a mad incomprehensible scramble, as if the ship were being taken by storm, an eastern mob swarmed up with all its goods and chattels. The little electric lantern suspended above the gangplank shone with a stark brilliance upon the dense, disorderly line of fezes and turbans that poked out from a sea of Caucasian hoods, lighting up staring eyes, thrusting shoulders, and hands clawing desperately at the handrail: and the same din resounded below, upon the very bottom steps which every few minutes would be swamped by a wave; there the crowd also fought and yelled, stumbling and clinging on, the thud of oars was heard, and boats packed with people bumped into each other again and again – first carried high on the crest of a wave, then plunging deep to disappear below the side. And the porpoise-like hulk of the ship rolled resiliently from side to side as if on a tight elastic band.

At last it began to grow quiet.

A very upright, square-shouldered gentleman, who had been one of the last to come aboard, surrendered his bag and ticket to a steward standing near the first-class deck-house and, having established that there were no empty cabins, made his way to the stern. Here where it was dark, he found several canvas deck-chairs, only one of them, it seemed, occupied by the shadowy figure of a man reclining beneath a travelling rug. The new passenger picked out a chair a few paces away. The chair was deep, and easing himself into it, he found that the sail-cloth moulded itself into a very snug and agreeable hollow. The ship rose and fell, turning and drifting slowly on the current. A soft breeze, smelling faintly of the sea, blew out of the southern summer night. And the night, quiet with the peace of summer, its clear sky filled with modest little stars, brought a velvety, transparent darkness. The lights in the distance were pale, and because the hour was late appeared to be drowsy. Soon everything aboard returned to normal, and voices issuing quiet commands and the rattle of the anchor chain could be heard . . . Then the stern began to shudder and there was a noise of screws and rushing water. Strung out in a low regular line along the distant shore, the lights began to move away. The rocking ceased.

Both passengers lay so motionless in their deck-chairs that they seemed to be fast asleep. But no, they were awake, staring fixedly at each other through the gloom. At last the first, the one whose legs were covered by a rug, asked in a calm, even voice:

'Are you going to the Crimea too?'

And the other, the one with square shoulders, answered in the same tone, taking his time:

'Yes, the Crimea and beyond. I'll stay in Alupka for a while and then journey on to Gagry.'

'I recognized you at once,' said the first man.

'I recognized you too at once,' replied the second.

'What a strange and unexpected meeting!'

'Yes, nothing could be stranger.'

'Actually, it isn't that I recognized you, exactly. It's as if I already knew somehow, in my heart of hearts, that you were bound to turn up, so I had no need to recognize you.'

'I felt exactly the same.'

'Really? How very odd . . . We have to admit to ourselves that there are moments in life which are – how can I put it? – well, just extraordinary perhaps. Maybe life isn't quite as straightforward as it appears.'

'Maybe. On the other hand there could be another explanation. We could have simply dreamed up this so-called premonition of ours on the spur of the moment.'

'Maybe. Yes, that's highly probable. In fact that's the most likely answer.'

'There you are, you see. We tend to intellectualize everything, while life itself is perhaps quite uncomplicated. It's probably like that scrimmage we've just seen on the gangplank. Where were all those fools rushing to like that, trampling each other into the ground?'

The two speakers remained silent for a moment. Then their conversation resumed.

'How long is it since we last saw each other? Twenty-three years?' asked the first passenger, the one under the rug.

'Yes, nearly,' answered the second. 'This autumn it'll be twenty-three years precisely. It's easy enough to calculate. Almost a quarter of a century.'

'A long time. A whole life-time. That is, I'm trying to say that both our lives are almost over.'

'Yes, yes. And what of it? Surely we're not afraid of the end?'

'Hm! No, of course not. Or hardly at all. It's all nonsense, the stories we tell to frighten ourselves. I mean when we try to put the fear of God into ourselves with the thought that life is drawing to a close and that in ten years or so we'll be lying in the grave. But just think of it: the grave. It's no laughing matter!'

'I agree. And I'd go further still. You're aware, I suppose, that I'm what's called a celebrity in the medical world?'

'As if there's anyone who doesn't know that! Of course I'm aware of it. And has it come to your attention that your humble servant, too, has made something of a name for himself?'

'But of course. I'm really quite an admirer of yours – a most avid reader,' said the second man.

'So here we are, a pair of celebrities. But what were you going to say?'

'Only that thanks to my eminence, or rather to a degree of knowledge which has no particular merit, but which is nonetheless fairly well-grounded, I know without a shadow of a doubt that I don't even have ten years to live, but only a few months. Well, at the very most – a year. It's been reliably established, both by myself and by professional colleagues, that I'm suffering from a fatal disease. And I assure you that I go on living almost as if there were nothing the matter. I just find it amusing in an ironic way: I wanted, if you please, to outstrip everyone in my understanding of the causes of death so that I could become famous and live a splendid life, and I got my wish at my own expense – I perceived my own death splendidly. They can fool you, trick you – come, come, old fellow, what the hell, we'll win through yet! – but in my case there's no room for tricks or lies. It's silly and embarrassing. So embarrassing in fact, that they tend to overdo the honesty, sprinkling it with maudlin flattery: Ah, well, esteemed colleague, it's not for us to pull the wool over your eyes. Finita la commèdia!'

'Are you serious?' asked the first man.

'Perfectly serious,' replied the second. 'And you know what the main problem is? Some Caius or other is mortal, ergo I too must die, but that'll be some other time. Well, in my case, unfortunately, it isn't quite like that: it's not some other time, but in a year. And how long is a year? Next summer you'll be sailing somewhere like this on the blue ocean while in Moscow my venerable bones will be resting in the Novodevichy Cemetery. So what does it all amount to? It amounts to the fact that I'm almost totally indifferent to this thought and that, worst of all, it isn't thanks to the sort of manly courage my students choose to see in me when I lecture them on my disease and its development as an example of clinical interest, but simply, you see, out of some idiotic lack of feeling. And knowing my fatal secret, noone around me feels anything either. Take you for instance – are you afraid for me?'

'Afraid for you? No, to be honest – not in the least, when it comes down to it.'

'And of course, you're not at all sorry for me?'

'No, I'm not sorry for you either. And yet you, I think, haven't the slightest belief in those fields of bliss where there's no sorrow and no lamentation but only the little apples of paradise.'

'Come now, what belief can you and I possibly have . . .'

And again they both said nothing for a while. Then they each took out a cigarette case and lit a cigarette.

'Mark you,' said the first man, the one lying under the rug. 'Neither of us is posing, neither of us is play-acting for the benefit of the other, or for any imaginary listener. We're talking to each other, I think you'll agree, in a very natural way, without any premeditated cynicism or that boastful irony which always contains some slight degree of compensation: here we are, we could be saying, just look at the fix we're in! Noone has ever known anything like it! And yet we're chatting away quite quietly, none of our silences pregnant with meaning or sage stoicism. Generally speaking, there's no more voluptuous animal on earth than man, man's cunning soul will always manage to find self-gratification in anything that befalls him. But in our case I don't see even a glimmer of this. And it's all the more curious since we have to add the peculiar circumstances of our relationship to our, as you put it, idiotic lack of feeling. We're very closely bound together, you and I. Or rather, to be more precise, we should be.'

'Indeed we should!' said the second man. 'When you think of the horror I must have caused you! I can imagine what you must have gone through.'

'Yes, but it was far worse even than you can imagine. Under any circumstances, that whole nightmare a man, a lover or a husband, has to live through when his wife has been taken, lured away from him, can never be anything but horrifying. You're left writhing every minute of the day and night in an agony of endless hurt pride, terrible jealous visions of the joy your rival is experiencing, and that hopeless, remorseless tenderness – or rather sexual yearning – aroused by the vanished female whom you long both to strangle with your bare hands and at the same time overwhelm with the most abject tokens of an obedience and devotion any dog would be proud of. It's all unspeakably dreadful. But to crown it all, I'm not like the man in the street. My sensitivity and imagination are highly developed. So you can imagine what I went through for years on end.'

'Really? For years?'

'I assure you, for no less than three years. And even afterwards, there was still that one thought of you and her and the intimacy you shared burning me like red-hot steel. It's quite easy to understand. Someone steals someone else's fiancée – all right, that's not too bad. But when it's a mistress, or as in our case, a wife! She with whom, excuse my frankness, you've been to bed, whose body and soul you know down to the last tiny detail, like the back of your hand . . . Just think what scope that provides for the jealous imagination! How can you survive her being possessed by another man? All this is more than human strength can bear. Why did I nearly drink myself to death, why was I broken in health and in spirit? Why did I miss the moment of the brightest flowering of my powers and talents? Without exaggerating in the least, you simply broke me in half. I grew whole again, but to what purpose? The man I'd been no longer existed and never could again. You'd reached into the holy of holies of my being. When Prince Gotama was choosing himself a bride and perceived Yasodhara who "had the form of a goddess and the eyes of a hind in spring", he performed God knows what feats because of her, battling with other youths – for instance, he shot an arrow into the air which was heard seven thousand miles away – and then taking a string of pearls from about his person, he wound it round Yasodhara with the words: "I choose her because we played in the forest together in the days of long ago when I was the son of a huntsman and she a forest maiden: my heart has remembered her." She was wearing a dark gold mantle that day and the prince glanced at her and said: "She wears a dark gold mantle because a myriad years ago when I was a hunter, I looked and saw she was a panther in the forest. My heart has remembered her." You must forgive me for all this poetry, but it contains a monumental, terrifying truth. Just consider those amazing words about a remembering heart – and then think of the horror when this, the most sacred of all earthly encounters, is destroyed by a stranger. Who knows, I too might have shot my arrow loud enough for it to be heard thousands of miles away – and then, suddenly, you appeared!'

'Well, and what do you feel towards me now?' asked the gentleman with square shoulders. 'Rage, contempt, a thirst for revenge?'

'Imagine: absolutely nothing. In spite of the tirade I've just delivered, absolutely nothing. It's terrifying, terrifying! There's how "my heart has remembered" for you! But you're perfectly aware of the fact that I feel nothing. Otherwise you wouldn't have asked.'

'Yes, you're right. I know. And that too is very frightening.'

'And yet we're not afraid. Total horror, and yet we're not frightened in the least!'

'Yes, I agree, not in the least. People say: the past, the past! But it's all rubbish. Strictly speaking people have no past. Just a sort of faint echo of everything they've lived by at various times.'

And the two men fell silent again for a moment. The ship was shuddering and steaming on: the calm sound of the sleepy waves streaming past her side came and went, a line spun, unreeling itself rapidly and monotonously behind the monotonously humming stern, and the ship's log on the end marked something off

now and then with a mysterious, silvery chime: brring . . . Then
the square-shouldered passenger asked:

'And tell me . . . What did you feel when you learned of her
death? Nothing then either?'

'Yes, almost nothing,' answered the passenger under the rug.
'Mostly a certain astonishment at my own lack of feeling. I
opened the morning paper and it just happened to catch my eye:
by the grace of God . . . We're not used to it, so it's strange to see
the name of someone we know, someone close to us, edged in
black in that fatal spot in the newspaper, printed in that large
ceremonious type. Then I tried to grieve; yes, I said to myself,
that's the same woman who . . . But

> Death's tidings came upon indifferent lips,
> Indifferently, I heard them . . .

I didn't manage to feel any grief at all. Only a kind of faint pity.
And she was the one whom "my heart has remembered", my
first, so cruel, so long-lasting love. I met her at the height of her
loveliness and innocence, at the height of that almost adolescent
trustingness and shyness which strikes so deeply at a man's heart,
because, perhaps, wherever you find femininity there must also
be this trusting helplessness, something child-like, a sign that the
young girl, the woman, always holds hidden within her the child
that is to come. After all, I was the first to whom, in a kind of
holy bliss and terror, she first surrendered all the gifts that God
had heaped upon her, it was her young virginal body, which I
would call the most exquisite thing in all the world, that I kissed,
truly a million times, in a fever the likes of which I've never
known again in all my life. And it was because of her that I went
mad, literally, night and day for years on end. Because of her that
I wept, tore my hair, contemplated suicide, drank, drove horses
into the ground, in my rage destroyed my best, perhaps most
valuable work . . . But twenty years go by – and I stare blankly
at her name in its funereal frame, blankly imagine her lying in her

coffin . . . The idea is unpleasant, but nothing more. I assure you, nothing more. But *you* now – especially now – do you feel anything?'

'Me? No – why conceal it? Almost nothing, of course . . .'

The ship steamed on; wave after wave rose hissing ahead of her, racing by with a splash, and a pale snowy path ran seething alongside, stretching behind the stern. There was a delicious breeze and a motionless pattern of stars stood on high above the black funnel, the rigging and the slender spike of the foremast.

'But do you know something?' the first man said suddenly, as if coming to his senses. 'Do you know what matters most? I couldn't in any way link her – the woman who died – with that other one, the one I've been talking about. Not in any way. Not in any way whatsoever. She was quite different, that other one, and to say that I felt nothing for her is a lie. So I haven't been accurate. I missed the point completely.'

The second man thought for a moment.

'And so?' he asked.

'And so almost the whole of our conversation can go by the board.'

'Oh, can it?' said the square-shouldered passenger. 'But that other one, as you put it, is merely yourself, your imagination, your feelings; in a word, part of you. So it follows that you've been experiencing all that emotion and agitation on your own behalf. Consider carefully.'

'Do you think so? I don't know. Maybe. Yes, maybe.'

'Well, and how long did it last, this agitation on your own behalf? Ten minutes? Let's say half an hour. Well, a day then . . .'

'Yes, yes. It's dreadful, but I think you're right. And where is she now? Up there in that beautiful sky?'

'Allah alone knows, my friend. Most probably, she's nowhere.'

'Is that what you believe? Yes, most probably that's it . . .'

The flat expanse of the open sea lay in an almost black circle beneath the airy luminous dome of the night sky. And lost in the middle of this round, dark expanse, the little ship held stubbornly and unerringly to her course. And, foaming lazily behind her, a pale milky path stretched endlessly into the distance where night melted into sea and where the horizon, in sharp contrast to all that milkiness, seemed dark and melancholy. And the log spun round and round on its line, mournfully and mysteriously marking something off now and again with its delicate, silvery chime: brring . .

After remaining silent for a while, the two men said quietly and easily to each other:

'Sleep well.'

'Sleep well.'

Alpes Maritimes, 1923

Mitya's Love

Translated by David Richards

I

In Moscow Mitya's last happy day had been the ninth of March. That, at least, was how it seemed to him.

He and Katya had been walking up Tverskoy Boulevard just after eleven. The winter had suddenly given way to spring, and in the sun it was almost hot. It was as if real larks had come and brought warmth and joy with them. Everything was wet and thawing, drops of water dripped from the houses, the yard-keepers were breaking up the ice on the pavements and pulling the sticky snow from the roofs, and the streets were crowded and bustling. The high clouds were dissolving into a fine white smoke and merging with the moist blue sky. In the distance Pushkin towered up in benevolent meditation, and the Strastnoy Monastery glinted in the sun. But the best thing of all was that Katya, looking especially pretty that day, had been a perfect model of artlessness and intimacy as she kept taking Mitya's arm with childlike trust and glancing up into his face, while he, happy almost to the point of arrogance, took such long strides that she could hardly keep up with him.

By the Pushkin memorial she had said quite unexpectedly:

'You're so funny and you've such a sweet, boyishly clumsy way of stretching your big mouth when you laugh. Don't get upset, it's that smile I love you for. And also your Byzantine eyes . . .'

Trying not to smile and suppressing both a secret contentment and a vague feeling of having been insulted, Mitya replied amicably as he glanced at the monument that now rose high over them:

'When it comes to boyishness, I don't think we're very far apart. And if I'm a Byzantine, then you're a Chinese empress. You've all gone simply mad over all these Byzantiums and Renaissances . . . I don't understand your mother!'

'Well, if you were her would you lock me up in a tower?' Katya asked.

'No, I'd simply lock the door against all that pseudoartistic Bohemian crowd, all those future celebrities from the studios and conservatoires and drama schools,' Mitya replied, still trying to keep calm and speak in an amicably casual tone. 'You told me yourself that Bukovetsky has already asked you to the Strelna for supper, and Yegorov wanted to model you naked as some sort of dying sea wave, and of course you were terribly flattered by the honour.'

'All the same, I'm not going to give up art even for you,' said Katya. 'Perhaps I am vile, as you often tell me,' she continued, though Mitya had never said this to her. 'Perhaps I am corrupt, but you must take me as I am. But don't let's quarrel, do stop being jealous just for once, it's such a lovely day! Can't you understand that all the same you're the best one for me, the only one?' she asked quietly and urgently, looking into his eyes with now feigned seductiveness, and then declaimed slowly and pensively:

'We share a dreaming secret,
As heart is pledged to heart . . .'

These lines had stung Mitya painfully. Overall, even that day there had been much that was unpleasant and painful. That joke of hers about his boyish clumsiness was unpleasant; he'd heard similar jokes from Katya before, and they weren't accidental. In one way or another, Katya often revealed herself as more grown-up than he was and frequently – without meaning to, that is, quite naturally – demonstrated her superiority over him, and he painfully saw this as a sign of her being somehow secretly and corruptly experienced. That 'all the same' was unpleasant – 'all the same you're the best one for me' – and her saying it in a voice suddenly lowered for some reason. But especially unpleasant were those two lines of verse, and her affected way of reciting them. However, even the verse and the affectation, that is, the very things which more than anything else reminded him of the milieu that was taking Katya away from him and that sharply incited his hatred and jealousy, Mitya bore relatively well on that happy ninth of March, his last happy day in Moscow, as it often seemed to him afterwards.

That day, on the way back from Zimmerman's on Kuznetsky Bridge, where she had bought several pieces by Skryabin, Katya had begun to talk about Mitya's mother, and said with a laugh:

'You can't imagine how frightened I am of her before I even meet her!'

For some reason, in all the time of their love they had never spoken of the future or what their love would lead to. And here was Katya suddenly speaking about Mitya's mother – and in such a way as if it was understood that she was her future mother-in-law.

II

After that everything seemed to go on as before. Mitya escorted Katya to the Art Theatre studio, to concerts and literary evenings, or spent the evening with her in her house in Kislovka, staying till two o'clock in the morning, enjoying the strange freedom given Katya by her mother, a chain-smoking, berouged lady with raspberry-pink hair, a pleasant, kind woman, long separated from her husband who had another family now. Katya also came to Mitya's room at his student lodgings on Molchanov-

ka, and as before their meetings were spent almost entirely in a
haze of intoxicating kisses. But Mitya couldn't help thinking that
suddenly something terrible had begun, that something had
changed, or had started to change in Katya.

How quickly that unforgettable, light-hearted time had flown
past, after they had just met, when, though barely acquainted,
they at once felt that they enjoyed nothing so much as talking just
to each other – from morning till night, if they could – and when
Mitya so unexpectedly found himself in that fabulous world of
love which he had been secretly awaiting since childhood, since
boyhood. That light-hearted time had been in December – a
frosty, serene December which had adorned Moscow every day
with thick rime and the dull red sphere of the low sun. January
and February had swept Mitya's love into a whirl of continuous
happiness already attained, or at least on the point of being
attained. But even then something had already begun – and ever
more often – to trouble and poison this happiness. Even then it
often seemed that there were two Katyas: one was the Katya
whom Mitya had urgently desired and wanted from the moment
they had first met, while the second was the authentic, ordinary
girl who painfully failed to coincide with the first. Even so,
nothing he had felt then could compare with what he was going
through now.

Everything could be explained. Spring had brought its seasonal
feminine concerns – purchases, orders, endless alterations to this
and that – and Katya really was often obliged to visit the
dressmaker with her mother. Furthermore, ahead of her lay her
exams at the private drama school where she was studying. And
so her preoccupation and absentmindedness could well be quite
natural. Thus Mitya constantly comforted himself. But the
comforting did not help, for what his mistrustful heart told him
to the contrary was stronger, and was confirmed more and more
clearly: Katya's inner inattentiveness to him was increasing, and
with it grew his own mistrustfulness and jealousy. The director

of the drama school was turning Katya's head with his praise and she could not resist telling Mitya about it. 'You are the pride of my school,' the director had said to her. During Lent, in addition to class work, he started also to give her private tuition so as to make an especially brilliant show with her at the exams. However, everyone knew that he seduced his pupils, every summer taking one of them off to the Caucasus, to Finland or abroad. And now it began to strike Mitya that for this summer the director had his eye on Katya who, even though it was not her fault, nevertheless probably already sensed and understood things and consequently already found herself, as it were, in a disgusting illicit relationship with him. And this thought tormented him all the more as Katya's attention diminished almost too obviously.

Something seemed to be generally distracting her from him. He could not think calmly about the director. And not just the director. It seemed that other interests had also begun to predominate over Katya's love. In whom, in what? Mitya didn't know, and he felt jealous of everyone and everything, but mainly of the life which in his imagination she seemed to have already begun to live in secret from him. It appeared to him that she was being irresistibly drawn away from him, perhaps to something that was too appalling even to contemplate.

Once Katya said to him, half-jokingly, in the presence of her mother:

'Mitya, you seem to look upon women like Domostroy does. And you'd make a perfect Othello. You know, I could never fall in love with you and marry you!'

'But I can't imagine love without jealousy,' her mother said. 'If there's no jealousy, there's no love, I always think.'

'No, Mama,' Katya said, with her usual propensity for repeating someone else's words, 'Jealousy means a lack of respect for the person you love. If I'm not trusted, that means I'm not loved.' She deliberately avoided Mitya's eyes.

'But I still think that jealousy *is* love,' her mother insisted. 'I've even read it somewhere – very well demonstrated, even with examples from the Bible, where God Himself is called jealous and vengeful . . .'

As for Mitya's love, it now expressed itself almost entirely in jealousy alone. And this jealousy was not a simple one, but somehow, it seemed to him, a special kind. He and Katya had not yet reached the final degree of intimacy, though they did permit themselves too much in the hours when they were alone together. And now during those hours Katya was even more passionate than before. But now even this had begun to seem suspect to him and at times roused terrible emotions in him. All the emotions that comprised his jealousy were terrible, but there was one among them which was more terrible than the rest and which Mitya was quite unable to define or even to understand. It was the feeling that those manifestations of passion, those very things which were so blissful and delightful, more elevated and beautiful than anything in the world when shared by him and Katya, became unspeakably disgusting, and even somehow perverted, when he thought of Katya with another man. He hated her violently then. Everything that he himself did with her when they were alone was for him full of heavenly charm and purity. But as soon as he imagined someone else in his place, everything at once changed, everything was transformed into something shameless which evoked a fierce longing to strangle Katya – and indeed her above all, rather than any imagined rival.

III

On the day of Katya's exam, which at last took place in the sixth week of Lent, the torment that Mitya was suffering seemed to be especially justified.

At the exam Katya simply did not see or notice him at all; she was a completely different, completely public person.

She was a great success. She was dressed all in white like a bride, and her nervous excitement made her quite lovely. Everyone applauded her warmly and affectionately and the director, a smug actor with dispassionate, sad eyes, sitting in the front row, made remarks to her now and again simply to assert himself, speaking in a low voice which he nevertheless somehow made audible throughout the hall and which sounded unbearable.

'Less like a reading,' he told her authoritatively, calmly, and as imperiously as if Katya were his private property. 'Don't act it, live it!' he articulated carefully.

That too was unbearable. And equally unbearable was the recitation itself which evoked applause. Katya's cheeks burnt hot from embarrassment, at moments her voice broke, she ran out of breath, and that was touching and sweet. But she recited with the cheap melodiousness, false emotion and silliness in every sound which was considered the height of artistic performance in that hateful milieu where Katya already belonged heart and soul. She did not speak, she exclaimed all the time with a sort of importunate, languid passion, and with an exaggerated, quite unjustifiably urgent tone of supplication, and Mitya did not know where to look out of embarrassment for her. The most terrible thing of all, however, was the mixture of angelic purity and depravity which she presented in her flushed face and white dress, which seemed shorter on the stage because everyone sitting in the hall was looking up at her, her white shoes, and her legs, sheathed in white silk stockings. 'The girl sang in the church choir,' Katya was reciting with an artificial, exaggerated naïvety about some girl or other who was supposed to be angelically innocent. Mitya felt both a heightened closeness to Katya, as one always does feel to a loved one seen in a crowd, and a malicious hostility; he felt proud of her, aware that after all it was to him that she belonged, and yet at the same time he felt a heart-rending pain – no, she no longer did belong to him.

After the exam, there were days of happiness again. But Mitya no longer had the same easy confidence in them. Recalling the exam, Katya told him:

'You're so stupid! Surely you knew that when I recited so well it was only for you?'

But he could not forget what he had felt at the exam, and could not admit that those feelings were still with him. Katya also sensed his hidden feelings and once, during a quarrel, she cried:

'I can't understand what you love me for if you think everything's so bad in me! What do you want of me anyway?'

But he himself could not understand what he loved her for, although he was aware that his love, far from diminishing, was growing ever stronger as he waged his jealous struggle against someone or something because of her, because of this love, because of its mounting intensity and its ever-increasing demands.

'You love only my body, not my soul,' Katya told him bitterly on one occasion.

Again these were someone else's theatrical words, but for all their silliness and triteness they touched upon something tormentingly insoluble . . . He did not know what he loved her for, nor could he say exactly what he wanted. What did 'love' mean, anyway? It was all the more impossible to give an answer to that question because the word 'love' had never received an exact definition in anything Mitya had ever heard or read about it. In books and in life everyone seemed to have made an agreement for all time to speak either exclusively of some sort of incorporeal love, or exclusively of what was called passion or sensuality. But his love was not like either. What did he feel for her? What was called love, or what was called passion? Was it Katya's soul, or her body that drove him almost to the point of fainting, to an agony of bliss, when he unbuttoned her blouse and kissed her breasts which were paradisically lovely and virginal and which she revealed with a kind of soul-shattering submissiveness and the shamelessness of the purest innocence?

IV

She was changing more and more.

Success in the exam played a large part in this. Yet there were other reasons too.

With the coming of spring Katya somehow immediately turned into a young society lady, all dressed up and always hurrying somewhere. Mitya now felt thoroughly ashamed of his dark corridor whenever she came to his lodgings – she always arrived in a cab now, never on foot – and walked swiftly down this corridor with her silk skirts rustling and a short veil over her face. She was invariably affectionate towards him now, but just as invariably she came late and cut short their meeting, saying that she had to go to the dressmaker's again with her mother.

'You know, we're buying clothes like mad!' she said, looking at him gaily with wide, shining eyes, knowing perfectly well that Mitya did not believe her, yet still saying it, since there was nothing to talk about any more.

She hardly ever even took her hat off now or let go of her umbrella as she sat aloof on his bed, driving him to distraction with her calves tightly sheathed in their silk stockings. And before she left, telling him that she would not be at home again that evening – she had to go off somewhere with Mama again of course – she invariably went through the performance that was clearly intended to make a fool of him and reward him for all his 'silly torments', as she put it: with a histrionically furtive glance at the door, she would slip from the bed, brush her thighs against his legs and say in a hurried whisper:

'Well, kiss me then!'

V

So at the end of April Mitya at last decided to take a rest and go away to the country.

He had completely exhausted both himself and Katya, and his

suffering was all the more unbearable because it appeared to be so groundless. What, indeed, had happened, what was Katya guilty of? And one day Katya said to him with the firmness of despair:

'Go away, yes, go away, I can't stand any more! We must separate for a time and clarify our relationship. You're so thin that Mama's sure you've got consumption. I can't take any more!'

So Mitya's departure was decided. To his great surprise, although he was beside himself with grief, he was almost happy to be going away. Once his departure had been decided, everything he had enjoyed before unexpectedly came back. After all, he still terribly wanted not to believe in the horror which haunted him day and night, and the slightest change in Katya was enough for everything to alter in his eyes. Indeed, Katya again became affectionate and passionate, now without any playacting – he felt it with the unerring sensitiveness of a jealous nature – and again as before he began to stay with her in the house until two in the morning, again they had something to talk about, and the nearer the day of his departure drew, the more ridiculous their separation and the need to 'clarify the relationship' seemed. Once Katya even burst into tears – normally she never cried – and those tears drew him terribly close to her; he felt a stab of acute pity for her and a sort of guilt towards her.

Katya's mother was leaving at the beginning of June to spend the whole summer in the Crimea and wanted Katya to be with her. They arranged to meet in Miskhor. Mitya was also supposed to come to Miskhor.

So he made his preparations for departure, and walked about Moscow in that strange state of intoxication which falls upon a person who is already gravely ill but cheerfully determines to stay on his feet. He was morbidly, drunkenly unhappy, and at the same time he was morbidly happy and touched by Katya's renewed closeness and her concern for him – she even went with him to buy the leather straps for his bags as if she were his fiancée or his wife – and generally by the return of almost everything that reminded him of the beginning of their love. And he perceived everything about him in the same way – the houses, the streets, the people driving or walking along, the weather clouding over as it always did in spring, the smell of dust and rain, and the church-like smell of the poplars breaking into blossom behind the garden walls in the side streets: everything reflected the bitterness of separation and the sweetness of hope for the summer and their meeting in the Crimea where nothing would stand in their way and everything would come true (though what he understood by everything, Mitya didn't quite know).

On the day of his departure his friend Protasov dropped in to say goodbye. Among senior schoolboys and university students one not infrequently encounters youths who have cultivated a genially gloomy and mocking manner and the air of someone older and more experienced than everyone else in the world. Such was Protasov, one of Mitya's closest acquaintances and his only real friend, who knew all the secrets of his love in spite of Mitya's secretiveness and reticence. He watched Mitya tightening the straps on his suitcase, saw how his hands shook, and said with a sadly wise smile:

'What innocent children you are, Lord forgive you! But for all that, it's high time you realized, my dear Werther from Tambov, that Katya is, first and foremost, a most typical female being, and that not even the chief of police himself can do anything about it. You, a male being, are going off your head, making the highest demands of the procreative instinct upon her, which is, of course, perfectly legitimate and in a sense even sacred. Your body is the supreme reason, as Herr Nietzsche has so rightly observed. But it's equally legitimate if you break your neck upon this sacred course. After all, you know, there are creatures in the animal kingdom whose fate it is to pay with their lives for their first and last act of love. But since this fate probably isn't absolutely inevitable in your case, keep your eyes open and look after yourself! In general, don't do anything hasty. "Cadet Schmidt, word of honour, summer will come back!" The world was not made in a day and Katya's not the only pebble on the beach. Judging by your efforts to strangle the suitcase, I see that you completely disagree, and that this pebble is a pebble after your own heart. Well, forgive me the unsolicited advice, and may St Nicholas and all his allies keep you safe!'

Protasov squeezed Mitya's hand hard and left. As Mitya tugged his pillow and blanket through the straps of his case the sound of singing rang through the window which opened into the yard. It was the student opposite who took singing lessons and practised from morning till night. He tested his voice and then began to sing 'The Asra'. Mitya hurried with the straps, buckling them anyhow, grabbed his cap, and went to Kislovka to say good-bye to Katya's mother. The tune and the words of the student's song echoed and repeated themselves so persistently in his mind that he saw neither the streets nor the passers-by, and walked more drunkenly than he had done on any of those last few days. It really did seem that Katya was the only pebble on the beach and that Cadet Schmidt was going to shoot himself with his revolver! Ah well, if she was, then she was, he thought, and his mind turned back to the song about the Sultan's daughter who used to walk in the garden, 'radiant in her beauty', and see a black slave, 'paler than death', standing by a fountain; one day she asked him who he was and where he came from, and he answered her, beginning ominously yet meekly and with gloomy simplicity: 'My name is Mohammed . . .' and ending in an exultantly tragic cry:

> 'I come from those poor Asras,
> Once we have loved, we die!'

Katya was getting dressed to go to the railway station to see him off, and called to him affectionately from her room – the room where he had spent so many unforgettable hours! – that she would be there before the first bell. The dear, kind woman with the raspberry-pink hair was sitting alone, smoking, and she gave Mitya a very sad look – she had probably understood everything long ago, and guessed what was going on. Blushing scarlet and inwardly trembling, Mitya kissed her soft, flabby hand, inclining his head filially, and she kissed him on the forehead several times with a mother's gentleness, and made the sign of the cross over him.

'"Oh, beloved,"' she said with a shy smile, as she quoted Griboyedov, '"Laugh as you live!" Well, God bless you, off you go, off you go.'

VI

Having got through all the last little chores which have to be done when leaving lodgings, with the help of the servant he stowed his luggage into a lop-sided cab, squeezed himself in beside it, started off and instantly felt that peculiar sensation which grips one when leaving a place – an era in one's life has come to an end (and forever)! – and at the same time a sudden lightness, a hopeful expectation of something new about to begin. He was somewhat calmer now, and looked about more cheerfully, almost with fresh eyes. It was the end. Farewell to Moscow and to everything he had gone through there! A light rain was falling, the sky was overcast, the side streets were deserted, the cobblestones gleamed darkly like iron, and the houses looked depressed and dirty. The cabman drove with agonizing slowness, and made Mitya time and again turn away from the street and hold his breath. They passed the Kremlin, then Pokrovka, and again turned down side streets where crows croaked huskily in the gardens, presaging rain and night, and yet it was spring, and the air smelt of spring. At long last they arrived, and at a run Mitya followed the porter through the crowded station out onto the platform and then onto the third line of tracks where the long and heavy Kursk train was already waiting. In the huge and disorderly crowd that was besieging the train, and over the heads of all the porters who were pushing clattering luggage trolleys and yelling warnings, he instantly singled her out as she stood 'radiant in her beauty', all by herself in the distance – a creature apart, not just in this crowd but in the whole world. The first bell had already rung – this time it was he who was late, not Katya. It was touching of her to arrive first; she had been waiting for him and rushed up to him, once again with the solicitude of a wife or a fiancée:

'Darling, go and get your seat quickly! The second bell's just about to go!'

After the second bell, she gazed up at him from the platform more touchingly still as he stood in the door of the third-class coach, which was already packed full and stinking. Everything about her was lovely – her sweet pretty little face, her small, trim figure, her freshness, her youth, in which femininity was still mixed with childishness, her uplifted, shining eyes, her modest blue hat which had a certain provocative elegance in the curve of the brim, and even her dark-grey suit whose material and silk lining Mitya in his adoration could almost feel. He stood there, thin and ungainly, wearing for the journey high clumsy boots and an old jacket with tarnished copper buttons. And yet Katya was gazing at him with an unfeigned loving and sad look. The third bell stabbed his heart so unexpectedly and harshly that he leapt down onto the platform like a madman; just as madly, and with an expression of horror on her face, Katya threw herself towards him. He pressed his lips to her gloved hand, jumped back into the coach, and through his tears waved his cap to her in frenzied rapture, while she gathered up her skirts with one hand and floated back together with the platform, still not lowering her uplifted gaze from him. She floated back faster and faster, the wind tousled Mitya's hair more and more fiercely as he thrust his head out of the window, the locomotive gathered speed ever more relentlessly, demanding its right of way with an insolent and menacing roar, and suddenly it was as if something had snatched away both Katya and the end of the platform . . .

VII

The long spring twilight, darkened by the rainclouds, had set in some time ago, the heavy train was rumbling across the bare, cool countryside – it was still early spring in the open country – the ticket-collectors were walking down the corridor asking for tickets and putting candles into the lanterns, but Mitya still stood beside the rattling window, cherishing the smell of Katya's glove on his lips, his entire being still aflame with the keen ardour of the last moment of parting. And the whole of that long Moscow winter, both happy and painful, which had transformed his whole life, rose up before him in its entirety, and already he saw it in a new sort of light. And it was in a new light that Katya too appeared before him. But who was she? What was she? And love, passion, soul, body – what were they? They weren't there, but something else was, something quite different. The smell of Katya's glove – was that not also Katya, and love, and soul, and body? And the peasants, the workmen in his coach, the woman taking her hideous child to the lavatory, the dim candles in the rattling lanterns, and the twilight in the bare spring fields – all of these were love, all of these were soul, and torment, and ineffable joy.

In the morning they reached Oryol, where he changed to the provincial train that stood waiting at a distant platform. And Mitya suddenly felt what a simple, calm and comforting familiar world this was compared with that Moscow world which had already passed into some fairyland whose centre was Katya, who somehow seemed now so lonely, so pathetic, and loved only with tenderness! Even the sky, painted here and there with the pale blue of rainclouds, and the wind here were simpler and calmer . . . The train set off from Oryol unhurriedly and Mitya sat in an almost empty coach, unhurriedly eating an embossed Tula honeycake. Then the train gathered speed, rocking and lulling him to sleep.

He did not wake till Verkhove. The train had stopped. The station was a fairly busy, bustling place, but also had a back-of-beyond air about it. Pleasant-smelling fumes came from the station kitchen. Mitya enjoyed a plate of cabbage soup and a bottle of beer and then dozed off again, overcome by a deep exhaustion. When he woke up again the train was racing through a springtime birch forest, which he recognized as being just before his destination. The spring twilight was gathering again, and the smell of rain and also, it seemed, of mushrooms came in through the open window. The forest was still quite bare, but the rumble of the train echoed more distinctly here than in the open country, and in the distance the tiny station lights were already twinkling with a springtime wistfulness. Now came the high green signal-light which looked especially attractive in the bare birch forest in the twilight, and with a clatter the train began to switch to another track . . . O God, how sweet and touching to see that rustic servant waiting for his young master on the platform!

The twilight and the clouds were growing darker as they drove from the station through a large village which was also vernal and muddy. Everything was enveloped in the incredibly gentle twilight, the profound silence of the earth and the warm night, which merged into the darkness of the indistinct, low-hanging rainclouds, and Mitya marvelled happily again: how calm, simple and humble was the village with its smelly, chimneyless cottages, long locked in sleep – good people don't light fires after Annunciation – and how good it was in this dark and warm steppe world! The tarantas jolted over the ruts in the muddy road, and the tall oak-trees behind a wealthy peasant's homestead towered up, still quite bare and bleak, with dark rooks' nests in their branches. At the cottage door a peasant stood peering into the dusk, a strange figure who might have come from ancient times: barefooted, he wore a tattered coat and a sheepskin hat on his long, straight hair . . . A warm, sweet, fragrant rain began to fall. Suddenly Mitya found himself thinking about the girls and young women sleeping in these cottages, about all that feminine world to which he had come close over that winter with Katya, and everything merged into one – Katya, the village girls, the night, the spring, the smell of the rain, the smell of the earth ploughed up and waiting to be fertilized, the smell of horse sweat, and his memory of the smell of the kid glove . . .

VIII

His life in the country began with peaceful, enchanting days.

That night, as they drove home from the station, Katya's image had apparently faded and dissolved in the surrounding world. But no, it only seemed so and continued to seem so for a few days longer while he caught up on sleep, recovered his balance, and adjusted to the newness of the impressions, familiar to him since childhood, of his home, the village, springtime in the country, and the vernal bareness and emptiness of the world, pure and young again in its readiness to blossom forth anew.

The estate was small, the house was old and plain, and the uncomplicated farm work did not call for a large staff. A quiet time began for Mitya. His sister Anya, a second-former at grammar school, and his brother Kostya, a young cadet, were not expected home from Oryol before the beginning of June when their summer holidays started. Mitya's mother, Olga Petrovna, was as always busy with the estate on which her only assistant was the steward (or bailiff, as the servants called him); she was often out in the fields and went to bed as soon as it got dark.

When the next day, having slept for twelve hours, Mitya washed, changed into clean clothes, came out of his sunny room – its windows faced east, over the garden – and walked through all the other rooms, he was suddenly struck by their comforting familiarity and a peaceful simplicity which soothed both soul and body. Everything stood where it had for many years and had the same familiar and pleasant smell. The rooms had been tidied for his homecoming, and all the floors had been scrubbed, though they hadn't quite finished the large dining-room which adjoined the front hall, or servants' hall, as they still called it. A freckled wench, hired from the village, stood on the window-sill next to the door that opened onto the veranda and was stretching upwards to reach the topmost pane which she polished with a swishing sound, while her reflection showed in the bottom panes, bluish and remote. Parasha, the housemaid, who had just taken a large washrag out of a pail of hot water, was walking white-legged and barefoot across the wet floor, balancing on her small heels. Pausing to wipe the sweat off her flushed face with the crook of her bare arm, she said to Mitya with a free and easy patter:

'Go and get breakfast, your Mama left for the station with the bailiff before light; you didn't even hear 'em, I'll be bound.'

And instantly Katya forced her way into his mind. Mitya caught himself lusting after that bare, feminine arm, after the feminine curve of the body stretching upwards to the top window pane, after her skirt and the sturdy, bare legs emerging from it like pillars, and he joyfully acknowledged Katya's power over him and his belonging to her, and felt her unseen presence in all his impressions of that morning.

And this presence made itself felt more and more keenly with every new day, and it grew more and more beautiful as he recovered his equilibrium, calmed down and began to forget the ordinary Katya who, in Moscow, had so frequently and so hurtfully failed to become one with the Katya created by his desire.

IX

This was the first time he had lived at home as an adult, treated even by Mama differently from before, but the most important thing was that he was living with his first real love in his heart, enjoying what his entire being had secretly yearned for since childhood and boyhood.

He had been only a child when he was first wondrously and mysteriously stirred by something inexpressible in words. One day – it must also have been in spring – somewhere in the garden near the lilac bushes (since he remembered the pungent smell of the blister beetles) at a very early age he had been standing with some young woman, probably his nursemaid, and suddenly something before him seemed to be illuminated with a heavenly radiance, perhaps his nursemaid's face, perhaps the sarafan on her full bosom, and a certain emotion had passed through him like a hot wave, stirring to life inside him, exactly as a baby stirs in its mother's womb . . . But that was like a dream. Like a dream too had been everything that happened afterwards, in his childhood, his boyhood and his school years. He would experience a special sort of rapture unlike anything else he knew over one or other of the little girls who came to his parties with their mothers, and with a secret, avid curiosity he would follow every movement of some small, enchanting creature, who was also unlike anything else he knew in her pretty party dress and slippers and with a silk bow in her hair. Later, when he was going to school in the town, he had been enraptured much more consciously and throughout almost a whole autumn with a schoolgirl who often appeared in the evening in the garden next door to sit in her favourite tree; her liveliness, her mocking air, her little brown dress, the round comb in her hair, her dirty hands, her laughter, and her loud shouts were all such that Mitya thought about her from morning till night, pining and sometimes even crying, ceaselessly wanting something from her. Then somehow this also had passed of its own accord and been forgotten, to be succeeded by new, longer or shorter, but still mysterious raptures, the keen joys and sorrows of momentary infatuations at school dances . . . his body full of vague longings and his heart holding ill-defined premonitions and expectations of something . . .

He had been born and brought up in the country, but as a secondary-schoolboy he always had to spend the spring in town, except for one year, the year before last, when coming back for Shrovetide he had fallen ill and stayed at home the whole of March and half of April to recuperate. It was a time he would never forget. He had been kept in bed the first two weeks, and only through the window could he see the sky, the snow, the garden, the tree trunks and branches changing every day alongside the growth of warmth and light in the world. He watched one thing after another. First, one morning it was so warm and sunny in his room that the awakening flies were crawling over the window panes; then in the afternoon of the following day the sun was behind the house, on the other side, the snow seen through his window had already taken on its springtime, bluish pallor, and the big clouds – white against the blue of the sky – seemed to rest on the tops of the trees; and then, a day later, there were such bright-blue gaps between the clouds and such a wet sheen on the bark of the trees, and the snow dripped so busily from the roof above the window that he could not tear his eyes away for joy. After this had come warm mists and rain, the snow melted and disappeared in a matter of days, the ice on the river broke, and the ground in the garden and the yard joyfully shed its covering and showed dark once more. Mitya was long to remember one day at the end of March when he had gone for his first ride into the countryside. The sky was not a vivid blue, but it glowed with such youthful vigour through the pale and colourless trees in the garden. Out in the fields the wind was still fresh, the stubble had a wild, rusty look, and where the earth was being ploughed – it was already being prepared for oats – the upturned oily black clods radiated a primordial power. He'd ridden boldly across the stubble and the upturned clods towards the forest, which he'd seen in the clear air from afar, bare, small and transparent, then descended into its hollows, his horse's hoofs swishing through the deep layer of the previous year's leaves, dry and pale-yellow in some places, wet and brown in others, and crossed the leaf-strewn gullies where there was still flood-water and where with a crack dark-golden woodcock flew out of the bushes right under his horse's hoofs. What had that spring meant to him, and especially that day out in the country when the wind had blown so freshly into his face, and his horse, after the hard going across the sodden stubble and the black ploughed fields, had breathed so noisily through its broad nostrils, snorting and neighing with such magnificent, savage strength? That spring, it had seemed to him then, was his first real love, it brought days of constant infatuation with someone or something, and he loved all the schoolgirls and all the village wenches in the world. But how remote that time seemed to him now! What a boy he had still been then, innocent, artless and narrow in his modest sorrows, joys and daydreams. His abstract, objectless love had then been but a dream, or rather a remembrance of some wonderful dream. Now, however, there was Katya in the world, there was a being who embodied this world and exulted over everything in it.

X

Only once during those early days at home was he reminded of Katya's existence ominously.

Late one evening Mitya went out onto the back porch. It was very dark and quiet and smelt of the damp countryside. Beyond the night clouds above the vague outlines of the garden tiny stars blinked tearfully. Suddenly out of the distance came a wild, diabolic hoot which turned into a squealing yelp. Mitya shuddered and went rigid, then cautiously descended the porch steps, went into the dark avenue which seemed to be watching him with hostility from all sides, and stood still again, listening expectantly. What was it, where was it, the thing that had so suddenly and horribly filled the garden with its cry? It was probably only a brown owl or a screech owl performing its act of love, he thought, yet his whole being froze as if at the invisible presence of the devil himself in that darkness. Then suddenly a rumbling howl which shook Mitya to the core resounded again, nearby in the treetops of the avenue, then came a creaking, rustling sound and the devil silently passed to another part of the garden. There he first gave a yelp and then began to moan and whimper piteously and imploringly like a child; he beat his wings, shrieked with agonized delight and began to squeal and break into lewd laughter that suggested he was being tickled and tormented. Mitya, trembling all over, strained eyes and ears into the darkness. Suddenly the devil's voice broke off on a sob, rent the garden with a wail of mortally languorous ecstasy, and then seemed to be swallowed up by the earth. Having vainly waited a few more minutes for further performance of this erotic horror, Mitya quietly went back home – and all night long he was tormented in his sleep by all those morbid and repulsive thoughts and feelings into which his love had been transformed that March in Moscow.

However, in the morning his nocturnal torments were soon dissipated by the sunlight. He remembered how Katya had cried when they firmly resolved that he had to leave Moscow for a time, he remembered with what rapture she had clutched at the thought that he too would come to the Crimea at the beginning of June, how touchingly she had helped him in his preparations for departure and how she had said goodbye to him at the station . . . He took out her photograph, and for a long, long time gazed at the small, elegantly groomed head, marvelling at the innocence and brightness of her direct, wide-open and slightly rounded eyes. Then he wrote her an especially long and especially warm-hearted letter which was full of faith in their love, and once again he was continually aware of her loving and radiant presence in everything he lived by and delighted in.

He remembered what he'd felt when his father died nine years earlier. That had also been in the spring. The day after that death, feeling bewildered and terrified, Mitya had walked timidly through the dining-room where his father, decked out in his nobleman's dress coat, lay on the table with his large, pale hands folded on his raised chest, his sparse beard looking very black and his nose white. He had come out onto the front porch, glanced at the huge gold-brocaded coffin lid which stood beside the front door, and suddenly felt the presence of death in the world. It was everywhere – in the sunlight, in the new grass in the yard, in the sky and in the garden . . . He'd gone into the garden, to the sun-dappled avenue of limes, and onto the side paths which were even sunnier, gazed at the trees and the first white butterflies, listened to the first, sweetly trilling birds, and he hadn't recognized anything: in everything he'd seen death, the terrifying table in the dining-room and that long, brocaded lid on the porch! The sun was not shining quite as before, the grass was not quite the same green, the butterflies did not hover quite as before over that spring grass which was as yet hot only on the tips of its blades – nothing was quite the same as the day before, everything had been transfigured as if at the approach of the end of the world, and the loveliness of spring and its perpetual youth seemed pitiful and sad. This feeling had lasted for a long time after that day, it had lasted all spring, as long as that fearsome, foul, sweetish smell lingered, or seemed to linger, in the scrubbed and frequently aired house . . .

Mitya was under a similar spell now, only it was a spell of quite another order: this spring, the spring of his first love, was quite unlike any spring he had known before. Once again, the world was transfigured, once again it seemed to be filled with something extraneous, but this time not with something hostile or horrible, on the contrary with something that fused miraculously with the joy and youthfulness of spring. And this extraneous something was Katya, or rather it was that most lovely thing in the world which Mitya wanted and asked of her. Now as the spring days unfolded he asked more and more of her. And now that she was not there herself and there was only her image, an image that did not exist, but was only desired, she did not in any way seem to disturb the purity and beauty of that which was asked of her, and with every day her presence became more and more vividly sensed in everything that Mitya's eye lit upon.

XI

He became joyfully aware of this during his very first week at home. It was only the eve of spring, so to speak. He would sit with a book at an open window in the drawing-room and look through the silver firs and pines which grew in the front garden, at the muddy little river in the meadow and at the village on the hillside beyond. In the bare branches of the ancient birches in the neighbouring garden the rooks were still cawing incessantly from morning till night (as they caw only in early spring), growing faint from their blissful diligence; the village on the hillside still had a drab, grey look, and only the willows were turning a yellowish green. He would go into the garden: that too was still stunted, bare and transparent – the only green was in the glades dotted with little turquoise flowers, though the acacias along the avenues had opened up, and a solitary cherry-tree in the hollow in the southern lower part of the garden had blossomed out in pale, small flowers. Or he would walk out into the country where the fields were still desolate and grey, the stubble still bristled, and the mud on the tracks across the fields had dried in mauve-coloured humps. All these things exuded the nakedness of young life, that time of expectancy, and all these things were Katya. And it only seemed that he was distracted by the village girls, hired to do various jobs in the house, by the workmen in the servants' hall, by books, walks, visits to peasants he knew in the village, conversations with Mama and drives into the countryside with the bailiff, a big, rough-spoken ex-soldier, in a racing droshky.

Another week passed. One night there was heavy rain but then immediately the hot sun seemed to come into its own, the spring lost its shy pallor, and everything around began to change not daily, but hourly. The stubbled fields were ploughed up and transformed into black velvet, the boundary-strips sprouted grass, the turf outside the house grew more succulent, the sky became a deeper and brighter blue, the garden quickly donned its new, soft-looking green finery, the grey clusters of lilac turned mauve and fragrant, and a multitude of large black flies, glinting a metallic blue, appeared on its dark-green, glossy leaves and in the hot sunspots on the paths. The branches of the apple-trees and pear-trees still stood out starkly, hardly showing their small, greyish and peculiarly soft leaves, but these apples and pears, stretching a network of their crooked boughs under the other trees, were already growing ringlets of milky snow, and with each day the blossoms became ever whiter, denser and more strongly scented. During this miraculous time Mitya watched all the springtime changes taking place about him with a joyful intensity. But Katya's image did not retreat or fade among these changes; on the contrary, she participated in them all and to all of them she imparted herself and her beauty, which flowered together with the flowering of the spring, together with that ever more luxuriantly white garden and the ever more deeply blue sky.

XII

One day, coming for tea into the dining-room which was flooded with the late afternoon sun, Mitya quite unexpectedly saw lying beside the samovar the mail which he had been vainly awaiting all morning. He quickly walked over to the table – Katya should have answered at least one of his many letters by now – and a small, exquisite envelope, addressed in her familiar cramped writing, glinted brightly and ominously before his eyes. He seized it and strode out of the house across the garden and into the main avenue. He went to the farthest part of the garden where the hollow ran across it, stopped, glanced around and quickly tore open the envelope. It was a short letter, just a few lines, but Mitya had to read it some five times before he took it in, so hard was his heart thumping. 'My beloved, my only one!' he read again and again, and the earth rocked under his feet from these exclamations. He raised his eyes – above the garden the sky shone with triumph and joy; all round him the garden itself shone in its snowy whiteness; a nightingale, already sensing the approaching cool of the evening, was trilling precisely, strongly and with the full sweetness of avian self-oblivion in the fresh greenery of some distant bushes – and the blood drained from his face as a prickling sensation ran across his scalp.

He walked home slowly – the cup of his love was full to the brim. And throughout the next few days he carried it within him just as carefully, quietly and happily awaiting another letter.

XIII

The garden was arraying itself in all manner of ways.

The huge old maple which towered over the whole southern part of the garden and was visible from everywhere looked even bigger and more conspicuous after donning its new green garb.

The main avenue at which Mitya was always gazing from the windows of his room also appeared taller and more conspicuous: the tops of its old limes, which were also covered, if only with an as yet transparent pattern of fresh young leaves, rose up and stretched like a pale-green ridge over the garden.

Then under the maple and under the limes lay a mass of curly, fragrant, cream-coloured blossoms.

And all this – the huge, luxuriant crown of the maple, the pale-green ridge of the limes, the bridal whiteness of the apple, pear and bird-cherry blossoms, the sun, the blue of the sky and everything in the lower reaches of the garden, in the hollow, alongside the side walks and paths and at the foot of the south wall of the house, the lilacs, the acacias, the currents, the nettles, the burdock and the wormwood – everything was astonishingly luxuriant and fresh and new.

The verdure advancing from all sides upon the clean, green courtyard made it seem more cramped, and the house had become somehow smaller and prettier. It looked as if it were expecting guests, for the doors and windows stood open for days at a time in all the rooms, in the white dining-room, the old-fashioned blue drawing-room, the small sitting-room which was also blue and hung with oval miniatures, and in the sunny library, a large, empty corner room with old icons in the corner facing the door and low ash bookcases along the walls. And everywhere the trees which had come up to the house, with their variously light- and dark-green foliage and the bright blue sky between their branches, gazed festively into the rooms.

But there was no letter. Mitya knew Katya's inability to write letters, he knew what an effort it always cost her to make herself sit at her writing table, find pen, paper and envelope, and above all not forget to buy a stamp and stop at a post-box. But once more, rational considerations were of little help. The happy, even proud confidence with which for several days he had awaited her next letter vanished, and he pined and worried more and more. For a letter like her first one had to be immediately followed by something even more beautiful and inspiriting. But Katya remained silent.

He began to go less often to the village or for rides in the countryside. He sat in the library leafing through magazines which had been lying in the bookcases for years, yellowing and stiffening. These magazines contained many beautiful poems by poets of old, with wonderful lines which almost always spoke of one thing, of that which has filled all poems and songs since the beginning of the world, which now nourished Mitya's soul too and which he could in one way or another invariably relate to himself, to his love and to Katya. And for hours on end he would sit in the armchair beside an open bookcase and with self-inflicted torture read over and over again:

'The world's asleep, my love, come into the shady garden.
The world's asleep, and none but the stars can see us . . .'

All these magic words and appeals seemed to be his own and addressed now only to her, to the one whom Mitya persistently saw in everything and everywhere. At times the appeal sounded almost menacing:

'The waters are smooth
Till the swans beat their wings,
Then the river is atremble.
See, the stars are bright
And the leaves are at rest,
O come, before the clouds assemble!'

Closing his eyes and turning cold, he again and again repeated this appeal, this call that came from a heart overflowing with the power of love, yearning for its triumph and for a blissful resolution. Then he would sit for a long time, staring into space and listening to the deep rural silence surrounding the house and shaking his head sorrowfully. No, she was not responding, she was sparkling silently, somewhere out there in that alien and remote Moscow world! And again the tenderness would ebb from his heart, and that menacing sinister incantation would resound more and more insistently:

'See, the stars are bright
And the leaves are at rest,
O come, before the clouds assemble!'

XIV

One day, having dozed for a while after lunch – lunch was taken at midday – Mitya left the house and walked slowly towards the orchard. Girls from the village often worked there, digging round the apple trees; and they were working there that day too. Mitya was going to sit by them and have a chat – something which was becoming a habit for him.

It was a hot, still day. He walked in the transparent shade of the avenue and looked at the curly, snowy-white branches all round him. The blossom on the pear-trees was especially dense and vigorous and the mixture of this whiteness with the bright blue of the sky produced a violet hue. The pear-trees and the apple-trees were flowering and shedding their blossom at the same time and the earth which had been dug up round them was completely covered with faded petals. Their sweetish, delicate scent hung in the warm air together with the smell of the hot, rotting dung in the cattle-yard. Occasionally a little cloud appeared, making the blue sky grow lighter, while the warm air and all the smells of decay became even more delicate and sweet. And the entire fragrant warmth of that vernal paradise was filled with the blissfully somnolent humming of the bees burrowing into that honeyed, curly snow. And all the time, in the blissful boredom of their day, the nightingales trilled, one after the other.

In the distance the avenue came to an end at the gate to the barn. To the left in the distance, in the corner of the orchard wall, was a black clump of firs. Next to these could be seen the bright dresses of two girls working among the apple-trees. As usual, Mitya turned off the main avenue towards them and, ducking down, made his way through the low spreading branches which brushed his face with a feminine touch and smelled of honey and also almost of lemon. And as usual, one of the girls, the thin, red-haired Sonka, let out a chortle as soon as she saw him and with feigned fright cried out: 'Help, master's coming.'

Jumping down from the thick pear-tree log where she had been resting, she rushed over to her spade.

The second girl, Glashka, on the other hand, pretended not to notice Mitya at all, and placing her foot firmly on the iron spade – she was wearing black felt half-boots which were full of white petals – she thrust it energetically into the ground, turned over the wedge of earth she had cut and began to sing in a loud, strong and pleasant voice:

'O garden, my garden, for whom are you blooming?'

She was a tall, rather masculine girl who was always serious.

Mitya went up to them and sat where Sonka had been sitting on the old pear-tree log which had been left to dry out. Sonka looked at him brightly and with affected familiarity and jollity asked in a loud voice:

'Just up then? Mind you don't sleep through important business!'

She liked Mitya and although she tried all she could to hide the fact, she failed and always behaved awkwardly in his presence, saying the first thing that came into her head but still always managing to hint at something; she was also dimly aware that Mitya's apparently absent-minded continual coming and going was not so straightforward. She suspected that Mitya was sleeping with Parasha, or at least was seeking to; she was jealous and spoke to him now softly, now sharply, and looked at him at times languorously in an attempt to convey her feelings, and at times coldly and with hostility. And all this gave Mitya a strange pleasure. There was still no letter, and now he was not living, but merely existing from day to day in a state of constant expectancy, languishing more and more through this expectancy and the impossibility of sharing with anyone the secret of his love and agony or of speaking about Katya and his hopes for the Crimea; consequently, he was pleased at Sonka's hints at some love of his, inasmuch as these conversations at least seemed to touch on that treasured secret which filled his heart with yearning. He was also moved by Sonka's infatuation for him, because it meant she was in some degree close and made her a sort of secret co-participant in the love life of his heart, and at times inspired the strange hope that he might find in Sonka some kind of confidante for his feelings or even a substitute for Katya.

Now Sonka, without realizing it herself, had again touched on his secret: 'Mind you don't sleep through important business!' He looked round. The dense dark-green clump of firs in front of him looked almost black under the brilliance of the day, and the sky displayed a particularly magnificent blue through their pointed tops. The young leaves on the limes, maples and elms, translucent from the sunlight which penetrated them everywhere, formed a light and joyous canopy over the whole garden and sprinkled a bright pattern of light and dark spots over the grass, the paths and the clearings; the hot fragrant blossom, showing up white under this canopy, seemed to be made of porcelain, and it too shone radiantly where the sun penetrated it. Smiling in spite of himself, Mitya asked Sonka:

'What important business could I sleep through then? The real trouble is I have no business at all.'

'Sh! Don't say too much. I'll believe you as it is!' exclaimed Sonka in response coarsely and cheerily, again giving Mitya pleasure with her certainty about his love affairs; then suddenly she gave another shout and waved her arms at a red calf with a curly white patch on its forehead which had slowly emerged from the firs, come up behind her and begun to chew the flounce of her cotton dress:

'Oi, give over! Lordy, you're a one, aren't you!'

'Is it true – they say they're trying to arrange a marriage for you?' asked Mitya, not knowing what to say but wanting to continue the conversation. 'They say it's a rich family and a handsome lad and yet you've refused, against your father's wishes . . .'

'Rich but stupid, dead from the neck up,' replied Sonka pertly, rather flattered. 'Perhaps I've got me eye on someone else . . .'

The serious and silent Glashka shook her head without pausing in her work:

'You want to keep quiet, me girl. You yap on without thinking, but people in the village'll start talking . . .'

'Shut up! Cut your cackle!' shouted Sonka. 'I wasn't born yesterday. I can look after meself.'

'Well, who's the someone else you've got your eye on then?' asked Mitya.

'Right, I confess!' said Sonka. 'I've fallen for your old shepherd. Whenever I see 'im I go hot all over. I ride old horses as well as you,' she said challengingly, obviously hinting at Parasha, who at the age of twenty was already regarded as an old maid in the village. And suddenly throwing down her spade with a liberty which her secret infatuation with the young master seemed to give her some right to, she sat down on the ground, stretched out her legs in their coarse old half-length boots and motley woollen stockings, and let her arms fall limply at her sides.

'Help, I've not done nothing, but I'm fair worn out,' she cried with a laugh and began to sing in a shrill voice:

> 'Me boots are in holes
> Though their toes are still shiny . . .'

and again she cried with a laugh:

'Come and have a rest in the hut with me, I'm ready for anything.'

Her laugh infected Mitya, and with a broad but awkward smile he jumped down from the branch, went over to Sonka and lay down with his head on her knees. She pushed him off, but he put

his head back again, thinking in the words of one of the poems in
which he had recently immersed himself:

> 'I see, o rose, the power of joy
> Her bright scroll deploy
> And wet it with dew –
> Unbounded and blind,
> Fragrant and kind,
> Love's realm lies in view . . .'

'Don't touch me!' cried Sonka, this time with genuine fright, as
she tried to lift his head away. 'Else I'll shout out so loud it'll
make all the wolves in the forest howl. I don't feel nothing for
you. There was something, but it's gone.'

Mitya shut his eyes and said nothing. The sun-light filtering
through the leaves, branches and blossom of the pear-tree
dappled his face and made it prickle with the heat. Sonka gave his
thick black hair an affectionately malicious tug.

'Just like a horse!' she cried, and pushed his cap down over his
eyes. Under the back of his head he could feel her legs – that most
awesome thing in the world, a woman's legs – then he wriggled
his head up to her stomach and caught the smell of her cotton
skirt and blouse, and it all blended with the blossoming garden
and with Katya; the languorous trill of the nightingales both in
the distance and close at hand, the continuous, drowsily volup-
tuous buzzing of innumerable bees, the honeyed warm air and
even simply the feel of the earth under his back filled him with
yearning for some superhuman happiness. Suddenly there was a
rustling sound in the firs, followed by a cheerfully gloating
chortle and a resounding 'Cuckoo, cuckoo!' – eerie, distinct, and
so close that he could hear the whirring of the creature's sharp
little tongue, and the desire for Katya, the desire and the
imperative need that she should at all costs immediately grant
him that superhuman happiness, seized Mitya so violently that to

Sonka's extreme astonishment he abruptly jumped up and mar-
ched away with giant strides.

Alongside that violent desire, that urgent need for happiness,
and at the sound of that resonant voice which had echoed with
such terrible distinctness directly over his head in the firs and
seemed to split asunder the entire vernal world, Mitya had
suddenly realized that there would not and could not be any
letter, that in Moscow something had happened, or was just
about to happen, and that he himself was done for, beyond all
hope.

XV

In the house he stopped for a moment before the mirror in the
hall.

'She's right,' he thought. 'Even if my eyes aren't quite Byzan-
tine, they're certainly like a madman's. And look at your
thinness, your uncouth bony awkwardness, your pitch-black
eyebrows and that thick black hair – really almost like a horse's,
just as Sonka said!'

But just then he heard the patter of bare feet behind him. He
felt embarrassed and turned round.

'Must be in love, always looking in the mirror,' said Parasha in
an affectionately teasing tone as she hurried past onto the
veranda, carrying a steaming samovar.

'Your Mama was looking for you,' she added, placing the
samovar heavily on the table which was set for tea, and turning
round she shot a quick sharp glance at Mitya.

'They all know, they've all guessed!' thought Mitya and only
just found the strength to ask:

'Where is she?'

'In her room.'

The sun which had travelled right round the house and was
already entering the western sky looked like a mirror as it peeped

through the pines and silver firs which shielded the veranda with their needled branches. The spindle-trees at their feet also shone with a summery glassiness. The table was in the shade, but patches of hot sunlight made the tablecloth gleam. Wasps were hovering over the little basket of white bread, the cut-glass bowl of jam and the teacups. The whole picture betokened a beautiful summer in the country and the possibility of being happy and carefree. In order to forestall his mother, who was of course no less aware of his position than the others, and to show her that his heart was perfectly free of burdensome secrets, Mitya went out of the dining-room and into the corridor off which led the doors to his room, his mother's room, and two others where Anya and Kostya slept in the summer. It was gloomy in the corridor, and his mother's room was enveloped in a bluish light. The room was comfortably cluttered with the most old-fashioned furniture in the house – chiffoniers, chests of drawers, a large bed and an icon-stand which usually had a lamp burning in front of it even though Olga Petrovna was not especially religious. Outside the open windows a broad shadow lay across the neglected flower-bed by the entrance to the main avenue; beyond the shadow the sun shone straight onto the garden which was a festive blaze of green and white. Olga Petrovna, a tall, thin, dark and serious woman of forty, was sitting in an armchair by the window; she didn't even glance at the long familiar view, but kept her bespectacled eyes fixed on her work as she quickly twisted her crochet-hook in and out.

'Were you looking for me, Mama?' asked Mitya, entering her room, but stopping just inside the door.

'Not really, I just wanted to see you. After all, I hardly ever see you nowadays except at dinner,' replied Olga Petrovna, without pausing in her crochet-work, and in a special, exaggeratedly calm tone.

Mitya recalled how on the ninth of March Katya had said that for some reason she was afraid of his mother, and recalled the secret and magical significance he had read into those words.

He muttered awkwardly:

'Perhaps you wanted to tell me something?'

'No, nothing, except that you seem to have been rather depressed these last few days,' said Olga Petrovna. 'Perhaps you should go off somewhere, to the Meshcherskys' for instance? . . . Their house is full of girls,' she added with a smile. 'And altogether I think they're a very nice, warm family.'

'I'd like to go and see them sometime soon,' Mitya answered with an effort. 'But let's have tea. It's so nice on the veranda . . . And we can have a chat there,' he added, knowing full well that his mother was too perceptive and too reticent to return to that unproductive conversation.

They stayed sitting on the veranda almost till sunset. After tea Mama carried on with her crochet-work and chatted about the neighbours and household affairs and about Anya and Kostya. (Anya again had to resit an examination in August). Mitya listened and occasionally answered, but all the time he had a feeling rather like that he had experienced just before leaving Moscow, as though he were light-headed because of some grave illness.

And in the evening he paced non-stop back and forth through the house for about two hours, passing through the dining-room, the drawing-room, the small sitting-room and the library, right up to the latter's south window which stood open to the garden. Through the windows of the dining-room and the drawing-room the sunset glowed a soft red through the pine and silver-fir branches, and the voices and laughter of the labourers could be heard as they gathered outside the servants' hall for supper. Looking down the line of rooms and out of the library window, Mitya could see the smooth, wan blue of the evening sky and one high and motionless roseate star; against this blue the green top of the maple tree and the almost wintry whiteness of all the blossom in the garden made a picturesque show. But Mitya continued to pace back and forth, no longer caring how this might be interpreted in the house. He clenched his teeth so hard that his head ached.

XVI

From that day he stopped watching all the changes being wrought around him by the advancing summer. He saw and even felt these changes, but they no longer had any independent meaning for him; he enjoyed them only as a source of pain, since the more beautiful the summer became, the more painful he found it. Katya had become a genuine obsession. He saw Katya in everything and behind everything to the point of absurdity; and since each new day confirmed ever more dreadfully that she no longer existed for him but was in someone else's power and that she was giving to someone else her love and herself which were meant to belong exclusively to him, everything in the world began to seem pointless and painful, and the more pointless and painful it became the more beautiful everything was.

At night he hardly slept at all. The magic of those moonlit nights was incomparable. The milky-white garden lay completely silent. Weak from over-indulgence, the nocturnal nightingales sang guardedly, competing with each other in the sweetness and delicacy of their song, vying in purity, precision and resonance. And the silent, tender, pale moon hung low over the garden, invariably accompanied by an inexpressibly lovely gentle ripple of light-blue clouds. Mitya slept with his curtains pulled back, and the garden and the moon looked into his room all night. And every time he opened his eyes and glanced at the moon he would immediately utter to himself, like a man possessed: 'Katya!' and this with such rapture and pain that even he himself began to see it as ridiculous. How indeed could the moon remind him of Katya? And yet somehow it did, and most astonishingly of all, in some visible way! But sometimes he simply saw nothing at all, and then his longing for Katya and his memories of what they had shared in Moscow gripped him with such force that his whole being would shudder with a feverish trembling and he would pray to God – alas, always in vain – that he might see her beside him, on this bed of his, if only in a dream. Once that winter he'd been with her in the Bolshoy at a performance of *Faust* with Sobinov and Chaliapin. For some reason that evening everything had seemed especially delightful: the bright abyss yawning beneath them, already hot and scented from the throng, the tiers of red-velvet and gold boxes overflowing with brilliant finery, the pearly radiance of the giant chandelier hanging over that abyss, and the sounds of the overture issuing forth far below under the motion of the conductor's baton, now thunderous and demonic, now infinitely tender and sad: 'There was a king in Thule . . .' After the performance he had taken Katya home to Kislovka through the hard frost of that moonlit night, stayed in her room particularly late, turning quite giddy from their kissing, and come away with the silk ribbon which Katya used to tie her plait up for the night. Now, during these agonizing May nights, he reached the point where he couldn't think without a shudder even of that ribbon which now lay in his writing desk.

But during the day he would sleep and then ride to the village where the railway station and post office were situated. The days were still set fair. Occasionally there would be a little rain, even the odd thunderstorm and heavy downpour, but then the hot sun would shine again, incessantly doing its urgent work in the gardens, fields and woods. The garden was fading and shedding its blossom but on the other hand vigorously growing ever denser and darker. The woods were submerged in a sea of innumerable flowers and long grass, and the nightingales and cuckoos ceaselessly uttered their calls in the green and resonant depths. The fields had lost their bare look and were carpeted with a rich variety of fresh corn shoots. And Mitya took himself off for whole days to these woods and fields.

He was now too ashamed to hang about every morning on the veranda or in the yard, fruitlessly awaiting the arrival of the bailiff or one of the labourers with the post. And indeed, the bailiff and the labourers didn't always have the time to ride five miles on such trivial errands. And so he began to ride to the post office himself. But he too invariably returned home with no more than a copy of the Oryol newspaper or a letter from Anya or Kostya. And his torment began to approach the limit of his endurance. The fields and woods through which he rode so overwhelmed him with their beauty and happiness that he began to feel an almost physical pain in his chest.

Late one afternoon he was riding back from the post office through an abandoned neighbouring estate standing in an old park which merged into the birch woods around it. He rode along Table Prospect, as the local peasants called the estate's main avenue, which comprised two rows of huge black firs. Magnificently gloomy, broad and completely covered by a thick carpet of slippery russet needles, it led up to the old house at the end of its corridor. The dry, red, peaceful light of the sun, which was setting to the left beyond the park and the woods, cast its slanting rays through the fir trunks to illuminate the floor of this corridor and glisten on the golden carpet of needles. And such an enchanted silence reigned all round, with only one or two nightingales trilling from one side of the park to the other, there was such a sweet scent of fir and of jasmine which had grown up round the house on all sides, and Mitya suddenly felt such a great happiness – belonging to someone else, long ago – in all these things and all at once with such terrifying clarity pictured Katya as his young wife on that huge tumbledown veranda among the jasmine, that he himself was conscious of the deathly pallor that spread over his face, and in a firm voice which filled the whole avenue he shouted out:

'If there's no letter within a week I'll shoot myself!'

XVII

The next day he got up late. After lunch he sat on the veranda with a book on his knees, gazing at the print-covered pages and vacantly wondering whether to go to the post office or not.

It was hot, and pairs of white butterflies hovered in turn over the burning grass and over the spindle-trees which glinted like glass. He followed the butterflies with his eyes, again wondering:

'Shall I go, or shall I stop these humiliating trips once and for all?'

Rising into view up the slope, the bailiff on his colt appeared in the gateway. He glanced at the veranda and rode straight towards it. When he reached it he reined in his horse and said:

'Morning. Still reading?'

He grinned and looked round.

'Mama asleep?' he asked quietly.

'I think so,' said Mitya. 'Why?'

The bailiff paused and then said quickly and seriously:

'Well, young master, a book's all very well, but there's a time and a place for everything. Why d'you live like a monk? Aren't there enough girls around?'

Mitya made no response and lowered his eyes to his book.

'Where've you been?' he asked without looking up.

'Post office,' said the bailiff. 'And of course there weren't no letters there, just the one newspaper.'

'Why do you say "of course"?'

'Because, I mean, she's still writing, she ain't finished yet,' said the bailiff rudely and sarcastically, offended that Mitya hadn't responded to his words. 'Here you are, then,' he said, handing the paper to Mitya, then he tapped his horse and rode off.

'I will shoot myself!' Mitya thought resolutely, staring into his book but seeing nothing.

XVIII

Even Mitya understood perfectly well that it was impossible to imagine anything more absurd than that – to shoot oneself, shatter one's skull, immediately halt the beating of a strong young heart, halt thought and feeling, lose hearing and sight, disappear from that inexpressibly beautiful world which had only just revealed itself fully to him for the first time, deprive himself instantly and forever of any participation in that life which embraced Katya and the advancing summer, the sky, the clouds, the sun, the warm wind, the corn in the fields, the villages, the countryside, the village girls, Mama, the estate, Anya, Kostya, the poems in the old magazines and, further off, Sebastopol, the Baydar Pass, the sultry mauve hills with their pine and beech forests, the blindingly white, stifling highway, the gardens at Livadia and Alupka, the burning sand by the shining sea, sun-tanned children, sun-tanned bathing beauties – and again Katya in a white dress, under a parasol, sitting on the pebbles at the edge of the waves which were blindingly brilliant and evoked an irrepressible smile of sheer happiness . . .

He understood all that, but what was to be done? How could he break out of that vicious circle, in which the better it was, the more agonizing and unbearable? That was what was beyond his strength – that very happiness with which the world over-whelmed him and yet which lacked something absolutely indispensable.

Thus he would wake up in the morning and the first thing to strike his eyes would be the joyous sun, the first thing he heard would be the joyous, long-familiar peal of bells from the village church beyond the dewy garden full of sparkle and shade, birds and flowers; even the yellowish wall-paper in his room, that very wall-paper which had grown yellow in his childhood, was also joyous and lovable. But immediately a single thought would pierce his heart with rapture and horror – Katya! The morning

sun shone with her youth, the freshness of the garden was her
freshness, the merry, playful notes of the pealing bells also
reflected the beauty and elegance of her image, the ancient
wall-paper begged that she should share with Mitya that beloved
rural heritage, that way of life in which here on this very estate,
in this very house, his fathers and grandfathers had lived and
died. And Mitya would throw off his blanket, jump out of bed in
his nightshirt open at the neck, long-legged and lanky, but still
strong, young and warm from sleep, quickly open the drawer of
his writing-desk, seize the cherished photograph and fall into a
reverie as he gazed at it avidly and questioningly. All the
loveliness, all the grace, all the inexplicable, radiant and alluring
aura of maidenhood and womanhood were expressed in that
small, rather serpentine head, in the cut of the hair and in the
slightly provocative but still innocent gaze! But that gaze stared
out enigmatically and radiated an unconquerable, cheerful si-
lence, and where could he find the strength to withstand it, so
close and yet so faraway, and now perhaps indeed lost for ever
after revealing the inexpressible happiness of being alive only to
deceive so shamelessly and terribly?

That evening when he had ridden back from the post office via
Shakhovskoye, that ancient, deserted estate with the black ave-
nue of firs, his impulsive exclamation had very accurately ex-
pressed the state of extreme prostration he had reached. Reining
in his horse at the post office window and looking down from the
saddle as the postmaster vainly rummaged through a heap of
newspapers and letters, he had suddenly heard behind him the
noise of a train approaching the station, and this noise together
with the smell of steam from the engine gave him a jolt of
happiness as he recalled the Kursk Station and Moscow in
general. As he rode home from the post office through the village
he had passed several stocky girls, and in the way each one moved
her hips he had recognized with a start something of Katya. In
the open countryside a troika of horses had galloped towards him

and in the tarantas which they were drawing he had caught a glimpse of two little hats, one of them a girl's, and he had almost cried out: 'Katya!' The white flowers on the verge were instantly associated in his mind with her white gloves and the blue mullein with the colour of her veil. And when he rode into Shakhovskoye at sunset the dry, sweet smell of the firs and the luxuriant aroma of the jasmine had given him such a vivid sense of summer and of some past, old-world summer life on that rich and beautiful estate that as he looked at the golden-red evening light in the avenue, at the house standing at the far end in the shade of the evening, he had suddenly seen Katya, in the full bloom of feminine loveliness, descending from the veranda into the garden, almost as distinctly as he saw the house and the jasmine. He had long lost any realistic image of her and with every day she had been appearing to him in ever more extraordinary, ever more transfigured guises. That evening, however, her transfiguration had achieved such power and such victorious triumph that Mitya was even more horrified than he had been on the afternoon when the cuckoo had uttered its cry above him.

XIX

He stopped going to the post office, forcing himself to break off the trips through a desperate, supreme effort of will. He also stopped writing. After all, he'd tried everything, written everything – furious protestations of his love, a love such as had never before been seen on earth, humiliating supplications for her love or at least her 'friendship', shameless fabrications about his being ill and writing from a sickbed, aimed at evoking a little pity or at least a little attention, and even threatening hints to the effect that there would seem to be only one thing left for him to do, relieve Katya and his 'more fortunate rivals' of his presence on earth. And having stopped writing and craving a reply, forcing himself with all his strength to expect nothing (and yet secretly hoping that a letter would come just at that moment when he'd either deceived fate by successfully pretending indifference or when he'd really achieved indifference), trying everything he knew to stop himself thinking about Katya and doing all he could to find salvation from her, he again began to read whatever came to hand, went about with the bailiff on estate business to the neighbouring villages, and repeated tirelessly to himself: 'It doesn't matter; what will be will be.'

And so, one day he and the bailiff were returning from a nearby farm; they were in the droshky and as usual driving fast. The bailiff sat in the front since he was driving, with Mitya behind, and both of them were being jolted up and down, especially Mitya, who kept a tight hold on the seat and stared, now at the back of the bailiff's red neck, now at the fields jumping up and down in front of him. As they approached the house the bailiff dropped the reins so that the horse slowed to a walk, started to roll a cigarette and said, grinning into his open tobacco pouch:

'You know, you shouldn't 'ave been offended at what I said the other day, young master. Wasn't I speaking the truth? A book's all very well, and why not read a bit on holiday? But it's not going to run away, you know; there's a time and a place for everything.'

Mitya blushed and unexpectedly found himself answering with feigned straightforwardness and an awkward grin:

'But I haven't found anyone . . .'

'What d'you mean?' said the bailiff. 'With all those girls around?'

'The young ones only lead you on,' answered Mitya, trying to assume the bailiff's tone. 'Not much hope there.'

'They don't lead you on. You just don't know the game,' said the bailiff, authoritatively now. 'And again, you're close-fisted. A dry spoon tears the mouth.'

'I wouldn't be close-fisted if the business was worthwhile and certain,' answered Mitya, suddenly shedding all embarrassment.

'Well, everything'll be all right then,' said the bailiff, lighting his cigarette and continuing in a somehow slightly offended tone:

'It's not your money or a tip I'm after. I just want to give you some pleasure. Whenever I look, the young master's depressed. So, I think to meself we must do something about it. I always consider me masters. I've been with you two years now and, thank the Lord, I've never had a bad word from you or the mistress. Others, for example, what do they care about their master's cattle? If they're well fed – good; if not – to hell with them. But it's not like that with me. With me the cattle comes first. That's what I tell the lads – think what you like about me, but I want the cattle well fed!'

Mitya had begun to think that the bailiff was drunk, but the man suddenly abandoned his confidingly offended tone and said, glancing over his shoulder inquiringly at Mitya:

'Well, which one could be better than Alyonka? She's a tasty piece, young, and her husband's away at the mines. Only of course you'll have to give her a little something too. Well, it'll cost you, say, five roubles in all. One rouble, say, to buy her a present, two in her hand, and well, something for me for my tobacco . . .'

'That's all right,' answered Mitya, again against his will. 'Only which Alyonka do you mean?'

'The forester's Alyonka, of course,' said the bailiff. 'Surely you know her? Married to the new forester's son. I think you saw her in church last Sunday. It struck me there and then – that's the one for our young master! She's only been married a year, keeps herself neat and tidy . . .'

'Well, right you are,' answered Mitya, smiling. 'You arrange it.'

'All right then, I'll do me best,' said the bailiff, taking up the reins. 'I'll put it to her one of these days then. And meanwhile you keep your eyes open. Tomorrow she's coming with the other girls to fix the bank in the garden, so you come to the garden too.

And that book won't run away; you can read your fill back in Moscow . . .'

He tapped the horse, and the droshky again began to jolt and jerk. Mitya kept a tight hold on the seat and, trying to avoid looking at the bailiff's fat red neck, gazed at the water-meadows in the distance beyond the trees in his garden and the willows of the village on the slope leading down to the river. Something absurdly unexpected and ridiculous but which at the same time sent a languorous shiver running through his whole body was already half-accomplished. And already there was something different about the long-familiar bell-tower which rose up before him over the tops of the trees in the garden with its cross glinting in the late afternoon sun.

XX

Because he was so lanky the village girls had nicknamed Mitya 'Borzoy'. He was one of those people with black, seemingly always wide-open eyes who even in maturity have neither moustache nor beard, but merely a sparse curly wiry fuzz. However, on the day after his conversation with the bailiff he had an early morning shave and put on a yellow silk shirt, which threw a strange but handsome light onto his strained and somehow inspired face.

Not long after ten, trying to assume the slightly bored air of someone going for a walk for want of anything better to do, he strolled into the garden.

He came out through the main porch which faced north. A slate-grey murkiness hung over the roofs of the coachhouse and the cattle-yard and over the part of the garden which looked towards the bell-tower. Indeed, everything looked grey, while strong-smelling smoke from the chimney of the servants' hall hung in the air. Mitya walked round the house and towards the avenue of limes, looking at the tops of the trees in the garden and at the sky. A hot breeze was blowing from the south-east where a few vague clouds were gathering beyond the garden. No birds sang; even the nightingales were silent. Only the bees in great numbers flew silently over the garden from their honey-gathering.

The girls mending the bank were again working by the clump of firs. To fill in the breach which the cattle had made they were using earth and the steaming, pleasantly fetid manure which the labourers kept carting to them from the cattle-yard via the avenue, which in consequence was strewn along its entire length with shiny moist droppings. There were six girls. Sonka was absent: she had agreed to marriage after all and stayed at home now, preparing for the wedding. There were three skinny little girls, there was the fat, nice-looking Anyutka, there was Glashka, looking even more severe and masculine than usual, and Alyonka. Mitya immediately spotted her through the trees, immediately realized it was she, even though he'd never seen her before, and was staggered at the quite unexpected resemblance she bore – or which he imagined she bore – to Katya. It was so striking that he even paused for a second, momentarily thunderstruck. Then he walked resolutely towards her, without taking his eyes off her.

Like Katya, she was short of stature and lively. Although she had come to do a dirty job, she was wearing a pretty, white cotton blouse with red dots, a skirt of the same material, a black patent-leather belt, a pink silk kerchief, red woollen stockings and soft, black half-boots in which – or rather in her small elegant feet – again there was something of Katya, in the mixture of the feminine and the childlike. Her head had the same smallness, and her dark eyes were set in her face and shone in almost exactly the same way as Katya's. As Mitya approached she was the only one not working, as if she sensed her special status among the others; she was standing on the bank with her right foot on a pitchfork, chatting with the bailiff. The bailiff lay under an appletree on his jacket which had a torn lining and was smoking, propped up on one elbow. When Mitya came up he politely moved over onto the grass, leaving the jacket for Mitya.

'Sit down, Mitry Palych – have a smoke,' he said in a friendly, casual tone.

Mitya shot a furtive glance at Alyonka – her pink kerchief threw a pleasant light on her face – sat down, and lowering his eyes lit a cigarette. (He'd given up smoking many times that winter and spring, but had now taken it up again.) Alyonka did not even give him a nod; it was as if she hadn't noticed him. The bailiff carried on telling her something Mitya didn't follow, having missed the beginning of the conversation. She was laughing, but in a way which suggested that neither her mind nor her heart was involved. The bailiff was speaking with a mocking disdain, inserting obscene hints into every sentence. She was replying lightly but also mockingly, implying that in his designs upon someone he'd behaved stupidly, much too high-handedly and at the same time like a coward who was afraid of his wife.

'Well, there's no out-talking you,' said the bailiff at last, breaking off the argument as if tired of its pointlessness. 'You'd better come and sit with us. The master wants a word with you.'

Alyonka looked away, pushed some dark curls back under her kerchief and made no move.

'Come on, you fool, I'm telling you,' said the bailiff.

Reflecting for a moment, Alyonka suddenly jumped lightly off the bank and squatted down two paces away from Mitya, who was still lying on the jacket, and cheerfully and curiously looked him straight in the face with her dark wide eyes. Then she laughed and asked:

'Is it true, young master, you don't sleep with no women, like a monk or something?'

'And how do you know he don't?' asked the bailiff.

'I just know,' said Alyonka. 'I've heard. But he mustn't. In Moscow he's got a . . .' and she rolled her eyes instead of finishing the sentence.

'There's no-one suitable, that's why he don't sleep with no-one,' answered the bailiff. 'A lot you know about his business!'

'What d'you mean, no-one?' said Alyonka, laughing. 'There's dozens of girls. Take Anyutka. Who could be better? Anyut, come here, there's a job for you!' she shouted in a ringing voice.

Anyutka, the girl with the broad fleshy back and short arms, turned round – she had a very nice-looking face and a kind, pleasant smile – shouted something back in a melodious voice, and set to work even more energetically.

'Come here, I'm telling you,' Alyonka repeated even more ringingly.

'No point. Not my game,' Anyutka sang out merrily.

'We don't want Anyutka, we want someone a bit neater, higher class,' said the bailiff authoritatively. 'We know who we want.'

And he gave Alyonka a very significant look. It disconcerted her somewhat and she blushed slightly.

'No, no, no,' she replied, covering her embarrassment with a smile. 'You won't find no-one better than Anyutka. But if you don't want Anyutka, what about Nastka? She keeps herself neat too – used to live in the town.'

'Well, that's enough, shut up,' said the bailiff with unexpected rudeness. 'Get back to work. You've talked enough nonsense. The mistress always tells me off as it is; she says I let you girls give me far too much cheek.'

Alyonka jumped up and, again with extraordinary lightness, took up her pitchfork. But the labourer who had dumped the last cartload of manure on the ground just at that moment yelled out 'Dinner!' and, jerking the reins, clattered off down the avenue with his empty cart.

'Dinner, dinner!' shouted the girls in various tones as they threw down their shovels and pitchforks, jumped over the bank or off it, exposing their bare legs and multi-coloured stockings, and ran to the clump of firs where they had left their bundles.

The bailiff looked at Mitya out of the corner of his eye and winked to indicate that the matter was advancing, then, getting up, agreed proprietorially:

'Well, if it's dinner, it's dinner.'

The girls, making a colourful sight against the black wall of firs, flopped down cheerfully on the grass, undid their bundles, took out the flat cakes they had brought with them, placing them on their skirts over their outstretched legs, and began to munch. They drank milk or kvass straight from bottles and carried on a loud, disorderly conversation, chortling over every word and every few minutes glancing at Mitya with curious and challenging eyes. Alyonka leant towards Anyutka and whispered something into her ear. Anyutka, smiling her charming smile in spite of herself, pushed her away with a hefty shove (so that Alyonka, choking with laughter, toppled over with her head on her knees) and shouted out with feigned indignation in her melodious voice which echoed round the fir clump:

'You fool! Why are you giggling at nothing? What's the joke?'

'We'd better shove off, Mitry Palych,' said the bailiff. 'The devil's really got into 'em today!'

XXI

The next day was Sunday, so no work was done in the garden. It had been pouring during the night, with the rain drumming against the wet roof, and the garden had been lit up again and again with a pale but extensive and fantastic light. Towards dawn, however, the weather had cleared, everything had again become simple and happy, and Mitya was awoken by the joyous, sunny pealing of the church bells.

He unhurriedly washed and dressed, drank a glass of tea, and set off for mass. 'Your Mama's already gone,' Parasha reproached him affectionately. 'You are a one.'

The church could be reached either via the pasture, by going out of the main gate and turning right, or via the garden and the main avenue and then along the road between the garden and the threshing barn. Mitya set off through the garden.

It was now high summer. Mitya walked along the avenue straight into the sun which was gleaming drily on the threshing barn and the field. And this gleam, and the pealing bells which somehow blended very well and peacefully with it and indeed with the whole of that country morning, and the fact that he had just washed, combed his shiny, wet black hair and put on his student's cap – everything suddenly seemed so good that even though Mitya had again not slept all night, once more going through a mass of the most diverse thoughts and feelings, he was suddenly seized with hope for the resolution of all his torments, for salvation and deliverance from them. The bells rang invitingly, the threshing barn ahead of him gleamed hot, a woodpecker stopped for a moment to elevate its crest and then quickly ran up the gnarled trunk of one of the limes to the light-green sunny crown, black and red velvety bumble-bees were busily burrowing into the flowers in the glades under the full glare of the sun, and the birds were trilling sweetly and lightheartedly all through the garden. Everything was as it had been many, many times in his childhood and boyhood, and he recalled all those lovely, carefree earlier days so vividly that all at once he felt confident that God was merciful and that it would perhaps be possible to get through life even without Katya.

'Yes, I really will go and see the Meshcherskys,' Mitya suddenly thought.

Just then he looked up, and twenty paces ahead of him he saw Alyonka at that very moment walking past the gate. She was again wearing her pink silk kerchief, but this time a pretty light-blue dress with frills and new, steel-tipped shoes. She walked quickly, her hips undulating, without noticing him, and he swiftly darted to one side, behind the trees.

Giving her time to disappear from view, he hurried back to the house with beating heart. He was suddenly aware that he had gone to church with the secret aim of catching a glimpse of her, and that seeing her in church was not permissible, was wrong.

XXII

During dinner a messenger brought a telegram from the station: Anya and Kostya announced that they would be coming home the next day, in the evening. Mitya felt quite indifferent to the news.

After dinner he lay on his back with his eyes shut on the wickerwork divan on the veranda, feeling the hot sun as it reached the veranda and listening to the summer buzzing of the flies. His heart was fluttering as an insoluble question filled his head – how on earth could he take further the business with Alyonka? When was it to be definitely decided? Why hadn't the bailiff asked her directly if she agreed yesterday, and if so, then where and when? At the same time another thing was tormenting him – should he or should he not break his firm resolve not to go to the post office again? Could he not go today just one more, one last time? Would that be a new and pointless mockery of his own pride, a new and pointless way of torturing himself with pathetic hope? But what could that trip – really just a little outing – now add to his agonies? Surely it was now quite obvious that everything in Moscow was finished for ever? What should he do now in general?

'Master!' a quiet voice suddenly called out by the balcony. 'Master, are you asleep?'

He quickly opened his eyes. In front of him stood the bailiff in a new cotton shirt and a new cap. His face was festive, satisfied and had a slightly sleepy, tipsy look.

'Master,' he whispered, 'Quick, let's go down to the wood. I've told the mistress I've got to see Trifon about the bees. Let's go quick, while she's resting, or she'll wake up and change her mind.

We'll take a bottle for Trifon and he'll get tight, you keep talking to him and I'll find a way to whisper to Alyonka. Come out quick, I've got the horses ready . . .'

Mitya jumped up, ran through the servants' hall, seized his cap and walked quickly to the coach house where, harnessed to the droshky, stood a fiery young colt.

XXIII

The colt took off and flew through the gate like the wind. Opposite the church they stopped for a minute outside the shop; they bought a pound of fat bacon and a bottle of vodka, and then galloped off again.

At the exit from the village Mitya glimpsed Anyutka standing outside her hut, dressed up but not knowing what to do. The bailiff shouted some jesting but coarse remark at her and with a needless, tipsy, malicious flourish gathered in the reins and with them gave the colt a thwack on the rump. The colt went even faster.

Mitya held on for dear life as he was bounced up and down. The sun was burning pleasantly on the back of his neck while the warm country air with its smell of flowering rye, dust and axle grease blew gently into his face. The breeze made the rye sway and sent a silvery-grey ripple through it as if it were some wonderful fur; every few minutes larks would rise up from it, sing, fly aslant and then descend; far ahead in the distance the forest stood out a soft blue.

A quarter of an hour later they were in the forest and still going fast, bumping over tree-stumps and roots as they raced along a sunny track which was bright with patches of sunlight and countless flowers in the thick long grass at the sides. Alyonka, wearing her light-blue dress and with her booted legs stretched straight out in front of her, was sitting among the young oak-trees which were coming into bud beside the cottage, working on some embroidery. Mitya was struck by the fresh, bitter smell of the forest and the new young oak-leaves and deafened by the resonant barking of the little dogs which surrounded the droshky and filled the whole forest with their yelps. They stood there, barking furiously at every conceivable pitch, but their shaggy muzzles were friendly and their tails were wagging.

They got down, tied the colt to a dry tree which must have been burnt by lightning, and went into the dark entrance.

The cottage was very clean and cosy and cramped; it was hot both from the sun which was shining over the forest through its two little windows and from the stove which had been lit that morning to bake bread. Fedosya, Alyonka's mother-in-law, a neat and handsome old woman, sat at the table with her back to one of the sun-filled little windows which was speckled with tiny flies. Seeing the young master, she rose to her feet and made a low bow. Mitya and the bailiff greeted her, then sat down and lit cigarettes.

'Where's Trifon, then?' asked the bailiff.

'Having a nap in the store-shed,' said Fedosya. 'I'll go and call him straightaway.'

'It's going all right,' whispered the bailiff, winking with both eyes, as soon as she'd gone out.

But nothing was yet going at all as far as Mitya could see. So far he felt only unbearably awkward – Fedosya looked as though she knew perfectly well why they had come. The thought that had been frightening him for the past three days again flashed through his mind: 'What am I doing? I'm going mad!' He felt like a sleepwalker subject to some alien will, moving faster and faster towards a fatal but irresistibly enticing precipice. But trying to appear calm and at ease, he sat and smoked, and ran his eye round the cottage. He felt particularly ashamed when he thought of Trifon coming in; he was, people said, a crabby and quick-witted peasant who would immediately see everything even more clearly than Fedosya. But at the same time another thought was also running through his mind: 'Where does she sleep, then? On that plank-bed, or in the store-shed?' It must be the store-shed, he thought. A summer night in the forest, windows with no frames or glass, all night the drowsy murmur of the forest, and she lying there sleeping . . .

XXIV

As he came in Trifon also bowed low to Mitya, but silently and without looking him in the eye. Then he sat down on a bench at the table and began to speak to the bailiff in a dry, hostile tone. What did he want? Why had he come? The bailiff hastened to answer that he'd been sent by the mistress, that she'd like Trifon to come and look at her apiary, that her beekeeper was a deaf old fool, whereas he, Trifon, was probably the leading bee-master in the whole province in intelligence and understanding – and he quickly pulled out of one trouser pocket the bottle of vodka and out of the other the bacon in its rough, grey, now grease-soaked paper. Trifon looked askance, cold and sarcastic, but got up from his seat and fetched a teacup from the shelf. The bailiff offered it first to Mitya, then to Trifon, then to Fedosya, who with pleasure drained it to the bottom; finally he poured some for himself. He drank it and immediately began to offer a second round, chewing a piece of bread and flaring his nostrils.

Trifon grew tipsy fairly quickly, but without losing any of his dry, hostile sarcasm. The bailiff became gloomy and sullen after the second cup. The conversation took on an outwardly friendly appearance, but the two mens' eyes were full of mistrust and malice. Alyonka did not show herself. Having lost all hope that she would come and seeing only too clearly that even if she did there was no counting on the bailiff's being able to whisper any 'little word' to her, Mitya stood up and announced sternly that it was time to go.

'In a minute, in a minute, no hurry!' the bailiff responded in a sullen and insolent tone: 'I must have another little word with you in confidence.'

'Well, you can tell me on the way back,' said Mitya calmly, but more sternly still. 'Come on.'

But the bailiff slapped his palm on the table and with a drunken mysteriousness repeated:

'But I tell you, it's not to be said on the way back! Come outside with me a moment . . .'

And rising heavily from his seat, he threw open the door into the entrance-hall.

'Well, what is it?'

'Keep quiet,' whispered the bailiff mysteriously, shutting the door after Mitya and swaying on his feet.

'Keep quiet about what?'

'Keep quiet!'

'I don't understand you.'

'Keep quiet. She's coming. Honest.'

Mitya pushed him aside, went out and stopped on the threshold, not knowing what to do. Should he wait a bit longer, drive off alone, or simply go home on foot?

The thick green forest stood ten yards away; it already lay in the evening shadow and so was even fresher, purer and more beautiful. Behind the forest, a serene pure sun was setting, filtering its guinea-gold rays through the treetops. And suddenly, from the heart of the forest, apparently far off, from the other side beyond the ravines, a melodious female voice rang out and reverberated, as alluringly and enchantingly as is possible only in a forest of a summer's evening.

'Hallo-o!' came the long-drawn-out cry, as the voice apparently amused itself with the forest echoes. 'Hallo-o!'

Mitya sprang forward and ran through the flowers and grass into the forest. The forest sloped into a stony gulley. In the gulley stood Alyonka, chewing a cowslip stem. Mitya ran to the edge of the gulley and stopped. She looked up at him with astonishment in her eyes.

'What are you doing here?' Mitya asked quietly.

'Looking for our Maruska and the cow,' she answered, also quietly.

'All right, will you come then?'

'Why should I come for nothing?'

'Who said for nothing?' asked Mitya, his voice now no more than a whisper. 'Don't worry about that.'

'So, when?' asked Alyonka.

'Tomorrow. When can you make it?'

Alyonka thought for a moment.

'I'm going to mother's tomorrow to shear a sheep,' she said after a short pause, peering warily into the forest on the slope behind Mitya. 'I'll come in the evening, soon as it's dark. But where? The threshing barn's no good, someone'll come in. What about the hut in the hollow in your garden? Only mind you don't cheat me, I'm not agreeing for nothing . . . It's not your Moscow here,' she added, looking up at him with laughing eyes. 'There they say it's the women what pay . . .'

XXV

The return journey was awful.

Trifon had not remained in debt but brought out a bottle of his own and the bailiff had got so drunk that he was unable to seat himself on the droshky at first attempt; instead, he fell across it so that the frightened colt started up and almost galloped off by itself. But Mitya sat in silence, watching the bailiff unsympathetically and waiting patiently for him to sort himself out. Again the bailiff whipped the horse along with absurd vehemence. Mitya remained silent, held on tight and stared at the evening sky and the fields jolting up and down in front of him. Above the fields to the west larks were singing their last brief songs; to the east, where the sky had already turned dark-blue ahead of approaching night, there were flashes of that distant, peaceful summer lightning which promises only good weather. Mitya took in all this evening beauty but it meant nothing to him now. There was only one thing in his thoughts and in his heart – the next evening!

At home he was greeted with the news that a letter had come confirming Anya's and Kostya's arrival the next day by the evening train. He was horror-struck – they would come home and run into the garden, perhaps to the hut in the hollow . . . But he quickly realized that they wouldn't get home from the station before nine and then they'd be fed and given tea . . .

'Will you go and meet them?' asked Olga Petrovna.

He felt himself go pale.

'No, I don't think so. I don't feel like it somehow. Besides, there wouldn't be a seat for me.'

'Well, you could go on horseback . . .'

'Oh, I don't know. Anyhow, what for? I don't really feel like it now.'

Olga Petrovna looked hard at him.

'Are you all right?'

'Perfectly,' Mitya replied almost rudely. 'I'm just very tired.'

And straightaway he went to his room, lay down on the divan in the dark, and fell asleep without getting undressed.

During the night he heard the sound of slow distant music and saw himself hanging over a huge, dimly-lit precipice. It grew lighter and lighter, deeper and deeper, more and more golden, brighter and brighter, and more and more crowded with people; and then, quite distinctly and with indescribable sadness and tenderness a voice rang out from the precipice and began to sing: 'There was a king in Thule . . .' Mitya shuddered with emotion, turned over and went to sleep again.

XXVI

The day seemed endless.

Like a robot, Mitya emerged from his room for tea and for dinner, then went back and again lay down; he turned to his writing desk and picked up a volume of Pisemsky which had lain idly there for ages, read a little without taking in a single word, stared for a long time at the ceiling, and listened to the smooth, satin, summer rustling of the sunlit garden outside the window. Once he got up and went to the library to fetch another book. But that room, charming as it was in its antiquity and with its calm atmosphere and its views – one window overlooked the beloved maple and the others the bright western sky – reminded him so vividly of those now infinitely remote spring days when he had sat there reading poetry in the old magazines, and suddenly seemed so poignantly associated with Katya, that he turned round and quickly walked back.

'To hell with it!' he thought irritatedly. 'To hell with all this tragic poetic suffering!'

With disgust he recalled his resolve to shoot himself if no letter came from Katya, lay down again, and again picked up the Pisemsky. But, as earlier, he took in nothing of what he read and at times, glancing at the book but thinking of Alyonka, he would start to shake all over from the gradually intensifying palpitations in his stomach. And the closer the evening approached, the more frequently he was seized by those throbbing palpitations. The voices and footsteps in the house and the voices in the yard – the tarantass was already being harnessed to go to the station – echoed as they do in times of illness when someone is lying by himself and ordinary everyday life carries on around him, indifferent to him and therefore alien and even hostile. At last Parasha called out from somewhere: 'Madame, the horses are ready!' and Mitya heard the crisp purling of the harness-bells, then a clatter of hooves and the swish of the tarantass as it rolled up to the porch. 'God, when on earth will this all stop?' Mitya mumbled, beside himself with impatience, lying still, but eagerly listening to Olga Petrovna's voice as she gave her final instructions in the servants' hall. Suddenly the harness-bells began to purl again, but then the noise of the coach rolling down the hill gradually muffled their sound until it faded completely . . .

Getting up quickly, Mitya went out into the dining-room. It was empty and illuminated by the bright yellow sunset. The whole house was empty, somehow strangely, frighteningly empty! With an uncanny feeling almost of farewell Mitya glanced through the line of wide-open, silent rooms, drawing-room, small sitting-room and library, through whose window he could see in the evening light the dark-blue southern horizon and the picturesque top of the maple over which, like a roseate speck, stood Antares. Then he looked into the servants' hall to see whether Parasha was there. Having made sure that that room too was empty, he seized his cap from the stand, ran back to his room and jumped through the window, his long legs landing far into the flower-bed. He froze there for a moment, then, hunched up, ran into the garden and turned off sharply onto an enclosed side path which was densely overgrown with acacia and lilac.

XXVII

There was no dew, and so the evening scents of the garden could not have been particularly strong. But in spite of the unreflecting nature of all his actions that evening, Mitya suddenly felt that except perhaps in his early childhood he had never known such a power and variety of scents as at that moment. Everything was fragrant – the acacias, the leaves of the lilac and the currant bushes, the burdock, the wormwood, the flowers, the grass, the earth . . .

Taking a few quick steps and wondering with a shudder: 'But suppose she lets me down and doesn't turn up?' – it now seemed

that his whole life depended on whether Alyonka turned up or
not – and catching among the scents of the plants the smell of
evening smoke coming from somewhere in the village, Mitya
stopped once more, and looked back for a moment: an evening
beetle slowly floated past, humming close to his ear, as if it were
spreading silence, peace and twilight, though light from the
early-summer sunset still filled half the sky with its even,
long-undimming glow; above the roof of the house which was just
visible through the trees the clear sharp crescent of the new moon
shone high in the transparent, empty heaven. Mitya glanced at it,
quickly crossed himself over the pit of his stomach and strode into
the acacias. The path led to the hollow, but not straight to the
hut, which was diagonally across to the left. Mitya strode
through the bushes and then began to run, ducking and pushing
away the low, wide-spreading branches. A minute later he was at
the rendezvous.

With trepidation he thrust himself into the hut's dark interior
which smelled of dry, rotting straw, and peered around with
searching eyes, satisfying himself almost with joy that she was
not there yet. But the fateful moment was approaching, and he
placed himself at the side of the hut, all his senses transformed
into concentrated vigilance. An extraordinary physical excite-
ment had gripped him almost every minute of that day. Now it
reached a peak. But strangely enough, both during the day and
now, it was somehow detached, it did not penetrate his whole
being; it possessed his body without moving his soul. His heart,
however, was beating wildly. And all around everything was so
astonishingly quiet that he could hear but one thing – that
beating. A few soft, colourless moths were silently and tirelessly
hovering and circling in the branches and in the grey foliage of
the apple-trees, sketching a variety of patterns against the evening
sky, and these moths made the silence seem even deeper, as
though they themselves were bewitching and enchanting it.
Suddenly somewhere behind him there was a crack, and the

sound shook him like a clap of thunder. He whirled round, glanced through the trees in the direction of the bank, and saw something black moving towards him under the apple boughs. But before he could gather his senses to ask himself what it was the dark object ran up to him and made a sweeping gesture. It was Alyonka.

She had been pushing back the hem of her short, black, home-spun woollen dress which she'd been holding over her head, and he saw her startled but smiling face. She was barefoot and wearing only the skirt and a plain, unbleached blouse which was tucked into it. Under the blouse her girlish breasts were taut. A wide-cut collar showed her neck and the beginning of her shoulders, while the sleeves rolled up above the elbow revealed her rounded arms. And her whole person, from her small head in its yellow kerchief to her little bare feet, which were feminine and childlike at the same time, was so pretty, so lithe and so captivating that Mitya, who until then had only observed her dressed up and now for the first time saw her in all the loveliness of this simplicity, inwardly gasped.

'Well, quick then,' she whispered merrily and furtively, and with a glance back over her shoulder she plunged into the scented dusk of the hut.

Just inside, she paused for a moment and Mitya, clenching his teeth to stop them chattering, hastily thrust his hand into his pocket – his legs were tense and iron-hard – and pushed a crumpled five-rouble note into her palm. She quickly hid it in her blouse and sat down on the ground. Mitya sat beside her and put his arm round her neck, not knowing what to do – should he kiss her or not? The smell of her kerchief and her hair and the oniony smell of her whole body, mixed with the smell of the hut and the smoke, were all so wonderful that Mitya's head spun as he took them in with mind and senses. And yet it was the same as earlier – a terrifyingly powerful physical desire which did not turn into a desire of the heart, into bliss, rapture and a languorous melting of the whole being. She leaned away from him and lay down on her back. He lay beside her, rolled towards her and stretched out his hand. With a soft nervous laugh she caught it and pulled it downwards.

'No, not allowed,' she suddenly said, half-jokingly, half-seriously.

She drew his hand away and held it tightly in her own small hand, while her eyes gazed through the triangular window-frame of the hut at the branches of the apple-trees, at the now dark-blue sky and at the motionless red dot of Antares which was still standing alone there. What did those eyes express? What should he do? Kiss her neck, or her lips? Suddenly she took hold of her short black skirt and said quickly:

'Well, get a move on . . .'

When they got up – Mitya rose utterly and completely disenchanted – Alyonka, adjusting her hair and tying on her kerchief, suddenly asked in an animated whisper, speaking now like an intimate friend or a mistress:

'People say you've been to Subbotino. Is it true the priest there's selling his piglets cheap? Have you heard?'

XXVIII

On the Saturday of that same week the rain which had started on Wednesday when it had poured right through the day was coming down in bucketfuls.

All day it poured even harder, unusually black and torrential.

And all day Mitya ceaselessly walked about the garden, weeping so bitterly that at times even he himself marvelled at the strength and abundance of his tears.

Parasha looked for him, shouting out in the yard and in the lime avenue, calling him first to lunch and then to tea, but he didn't reply.

It was cold, piercingly damp, and dark with rainclouds; against

their blackness the dense greenery of the wet garden stood out
especially thick, fresh and bright. The wind which blew up from
time to time would shake a second downpour from the trees –
whole cascades of droplets. But Mitya did not see or look at
anything. His white cap was drooping and had turned dark-grey,
his student's jacket was now black, and his boots were covered in
mud up to the knee. Dripping wet, soaked to the skin, ashen-
faced and with swollen, mad eyes, he looked awesome.

He smoked cigarette after cigarette, strode through the mud
along the paths or sometimes entirely at random, through the
long wet grass under the apple-trees and pear-trees, bumping into
their crooked and gnarled branches which were covered with
patches of grey-green, sodden lichen. He sat on the swollen black
garden-benches or went off to the hollow to lie on the damp straw
in the hut on the very spot where he had lain with Alyonka. The
cold and the icy damp air had turned his large hands blue and his
lips mauve, while his deathly-pale face with its sunken cheeks had
taken on a violet tinge. He lay on his back with his legs crossed
and his hands behind his head, staring wildly at the black straw
roof which was dripping heavy, rust-coloured drops. Then his
face twitched and his eyebrows started to dance. He impulsively
jumped up, pulling out of his trouser-pocket the stained and
crumpled letter he had received late the previous evening (it had
been brought over by a land surveyor who had come to the estate
for a few days' work); he had already read it a hundred times, and
now, for the hundred and first time, he avidly devoured it once
more:

Dear Mitya,
Don't bear me any grudges. Forget, forget everything there
was between us. I'm wicked, vile and depraved, I'm not
worthy of you, but I'm madly in love with art. I've made up
my mind, the die is cast, I'm going away – you know who
with. You're sensitive and intelligent, you'll understand. I

beg you, don't torment yourself and me. Don't write, it's pointless.

When he got to this point Mitya screwed up the letter, buried his face in the wet straw and, with teeth furiously clenched, choked with sobs. The intimate singular which she'd let slip into that last sentence was such a horrific reminder of their former closeness that it almost resurrected it and filled his heart with an unbearable tenderness. It was more than human strength could stand. And next to that singular, the firm declaration that even writing to her was now pointless! Yes, he knew that well enough – pointless! Everything was finished, finished for ever!

Just before dusk the rain, which had been coming down with tenfold force and accompanied by unexpected rolls of thunder, finally drove him back into the house. Soaked from head to foot and with his teeth chattering from the icy chill which enveloped his whole body, he peered out from under the trees and, having made sure that no-one would see him, ran across to the window of his room and pushed it up from outside – it was an old-fashioned sash window – climbed in, locked the door and threw himself onto his bed.

Darkness quickly began to fall. The rain was drumming everywhere, on the roof, around the house and in the garden. The drumming was of two kinds – the first in the garden, and the other around the house where it was accompanied by a constant gurgling and splashing in the drain-pipes as they poured water into the puddles. And in Mitya, who had immediately lapsed into a numb torpor, this evoked an inexplicable anxiety and, taken with the heat burning in his nostrils, his breath and his head, plunged him into a sort of narcosis, creating as it were another world, another early evening in what seemed to be another house which was full of a terrible foreboding.

He knew, he could feel that he was in his own room which was already almost dark from the rain and the advancing evening and that over there, in the dining-room, the voices of Mama, Anya, Kostya and the surveyor could be heard round the tea-table, but at the same time he was walking through another strange house, following after a young nursemaid who was gliding away from him, and he was seized with an inexplicable, gradually mounting horror which was nevertheless mixed with a lustful yearning and a foreboding of intimacy between two people, an intimacy which had about it something unnatural and loathsome but in which he himself was also somehow participating. And he felt all this through the intermediacy of a baby with a broad white face which the pretty young nanny, leaning slightly backwards, was carrying in her arms and rocking to sleep. Mitya hastened to overtake her and did so, and was just about to look into her face – was it perhaps Alyonka? – when suddenly he found himself in a gloomy school classroom with chalk-smeared windows. The woman who was standing there in front of a chest of drawers and looking into a mirror could not see him, since he had suddenly become invisible. She was wearing a yellow silk petticoat which clung to her rounded hips, high-heeled shoes, fine black fishnet stockings which her flesh showed through, and, deliciously shy and nervous, she knew what was about to happen. She had already managed to hide the baby in one of the drawers. She was rapidly plaiting a tress of hair which she had pulled round in front of her, and while glancing at the door out of the corner of her eye she was looking in the mirror which reflected her powdered face, bare shoulders and milky-blue little breasts with their pink nipples. Suddenly the door was flung open and a gentleman in a dinner-jacket with a bloodless clean-shaven face and short black curly hair came in, glancing round the room with an eerie confidence. He took out a slim cigarette-case and proceeded to light up with familiar ease. Aware of his purpose, she looked at him shyly as she finished plaiting her tress, then she tossed the plait over her shoulder and opened her bare arms. He condescendingly put his arms round her waist and she embraced his neck, exposing her dark armpits, clung to him and buried her face in his chest . . .

XXIX

And Mitya woke up bathed in sweat, with the shatteringly clear awareness that he was done for and that the world was so monstrously hopeless and dark that it couldn't be worse even in the inferno, beyond the grave. His room was in darkness, outside the rain drummed and splashed, and this drumming and splashing was unbearable, in its noise alone, for a body shivering all over with a chill. More unbearable and horrible than anything else, however, was the monstrous unnaturalness of human copulation, in which it seemed he too had just shared with the clean-shaven gentleman. From the dining-room came the sound of voices and laughter. They too were horrible and unnatural in their estrangement from him and in the way they reflected the brutishness of life with its indifference and mercilessness towards him . . .

'Katya!' he said, sitting up in bed and swinging his feet onto the floor. 'Katya, what's happening?' he said out loud, perfectly certain that she would hear him, that she was there, that she was silent and unresponsive only because she herself had been crushed and because she had understood the irreparable horror of everything she'd done.

'Oh, it doesn't matter, Katya,' he whispered bitterly and tenderly, wanting to tell her that he would forgive her everything if only she would run back to him as before, so that together they could save each other and save their beautiful love in that most beautiful springtime world which only so recently had been like paradise. But as soon as he had whispered 'Oh, it doesn't matter, Katya,' he immediately realized that it did matter, that salvation and a return to that wonderful vision he had once been granted in Shakhovskoye on the jasmine-bedecked veranda did not and could not exist, and he began to sob quietly from the pain that rent his heart.

That pain was so strong and so unbearable that without thinking what he was doing, unaware of what the consequences would be, and passionately desiring only one thing – for just one moment to rid himself of the pain and to avoid finding himself again in that horrible world where he had spent the whole day and where he had just lived through the most horrible and abominable of all earthly nightmares, he groped for the drawer of the bedside-table, opened it, seized the cold heavy lump of his revolver and, heaving a deep and joyful sigh, opened his mouth wide and forcefully, with a sensual delight, pulled the trigger.

Alpes Maritimes, 14 September 1924

Sunstroke

Translated by Sophie Lund

After dinner they left the hot brightly-lit dining-room and went up on deck, pausing at the rail. She closed her eyes, pressed the back of her hand against her cheek, and starting to laugh in an enchantingly simple manner – everything was enchanting about this little woman – said:

'I think I'm drunk . . . Where've you come from? Three hours ago I had no idea that you existed. I don't even know where you came aboard. Was it Samara? But no matter . . . Is my head spinning or are we making a turn?'

Ahead was darkness and lights. From out of this darkness a strong warm breeze blew into their faces and the lights went racing off somewhere to the side: with a fine Volga flourish the steamer described a precise, wide arc and headed for a small jetty.

The lieutenant took her hand and lifted it to his lips. Small and firm, the hand smelled of the sun. And blissfully, unbearably, his heart missed a beat at the thought of how firm and brown the rest of her must also be under her light cotton dress, after an entire month spent basking in the southern sun on the hot sand of the beach (she had said she was travelling from Anapa). The lieutenant muttered:

'Let's get off.'

'Where?' she asked, surprised.

'At this landing.'

'Why?'

He stayed silent. She again pressed the back of her hand to her burning cheek.

'You're mad . . .'

'Let's get off . . .' he repeated, dully, 'I beseech you . . .'

'Oh, very well, as you wish . . .' she said, and turned away.

Carried forward by its own momentum, the steamer collided against the dimly-lit jetty with a soft thud and they almost fell on top of each other. The end of a rope flew past above their heads and the engine went into reverse in a rush of noisily churning water and the rattle of gangplanks . . . The lieutenant dashed off to get their belongings.

In a moment they had passed through a sleepy little office and, having emerged onto sand deep enough to reach the hub of a wheel, silently took their places in a dusty cab. The long haul uphill past infrequent crooked lamp-posts, along a road which was thick with dust, seemed endless. But eventually they reached the top and turned, clattering, onto a carriageway which led them to a square with shops and offices, a watchtower, and all the balmy warmth and scents of a country town on a summer night. The cabby halted in front of an illuminated entrance where, beyond half-open doors, an old wooden staircase wound its way upwards, and an aged unshaven porter wearing a pink Cossack shirt beneath his frock-coat grumpily took their baggage and shuffled forward on flat feet. They were shown into a room which, although large, was stiflingly hot after baking in the sun all day, with filmy white curtains drawn at the windows and two fresh candles on the dressing-table – and as soon as they were inside and the porter had closed the door behind him, the lieutenant flung himself at her with such urgency, and they both lost their breath in such a frenzied kiss, that the memory of that moment stayed with them for many, many years to come: in all their lives nothing like it had ever happened to either of them.

At ten o'clock the next morning – a hot sunny happy morning filled with the sound of church bells, with a market in the square in front of the hotel and the smell of hay and tar and all the mingled aromatic scents which perfume the air of a Russian country town – this small anonymous woman who had never told him her name and had jokingly called herself the beautiful stranger, went away. They hadn't slept much, but in the morning after emerging from behind the screen which stood by the bed and spending five minutes washing her face and putting on her clothes, she was as fresh as if she had been seventeen years old. Was she embarrassed? No – only very slightly. As before, she was open and gay, and already being sensible.

'No, no, my darling,' she said in reply to his entreaty that they might travel on together. 'No, you'll have to stay here until the next boat. If we leave together everything will be ruined. I would find that very disagreeable. I give you my word that I'm not at all the sort of person you might take me for. Nothing remotely like this has ever happened to me before and never will again. It's as if I had a black-out . . . Or rather as if we both suffered some kind of sunstroke.'

And the lieutenant, cheerfully somehow, agreed with her. In a cheerful and happy frame of mind he accompanied her to the jetty – just in time for the departure of the pink-painted ferry – kissed her on deck in full view of everybody, and only narrowly succeeded in jumping back onto the gangplank before it was drawn away.

With the same cheerfulness and equanimity he returned to the hotel. However, something had already changed. The room seemed somehow quite different without her. It was still filled with her presence and yet it was empty. How strange! It still smelled of her expensive English cologne and her half-empty cup was still there on the tray, but she no longer existed . . . And all of a sudden the lieutenant's heart was pierced by a feeling of such aching tenderness that he made haste to light a cigarette and walk up and down the room several times.

'What a curious adventure!' he said out aloud, with a laugh, feeling tears welling up in his eyes. "I give you my word that I'm

not at all the sort of person you might take me for . . ." and she's
gone!'

The screen had been moved aside, but the bed hadn't been
made. And he suddenly felt that he could no longer bring himself
to look at that bed. He hid it with the screen, shut the windows so
as not to hear the hubbub of the market-place and the screech of
wheels, and drawing the billowing white curtains sat down on the
sofa. Yes, so that was the end of his 'wayside adventure'. She had
gone – and was now far away, sitting, he imagined, in the white
glassed-in saloon or on deck gazing at the vast river sparkling in
the sunlight and the rafts floating by, at the yellow sand-banks
and the distant, shining prospect of water and sky and all that
immeasurable expanse of the Volga. Farewell – forever and for all
eternity . . . Because where could they possibly meet again?
'After all, I simply can't,' he thought, 'I simply can't just turn up
for no reason in the town where her husband and her three-year-
old little girl live, where her entire family is to be found, the
whole of her everyday existence . . .' And that town suddenly
seemed to him a special, sacred place, while the idea that she
would go on living her lonely life there, often perhaps thinking of
him and their fleeting, chance encounter, when he would never
see her again, stunned and amazed him. No, it wasn't possible. It
would be too crazy, too unnatural, too unlikely. And there
seemed to be so much pain and futility awaiting him in the long
future of his life without her that he was engulfed by a feeling of
horror and despair.

'What the devil!' he said to himself, getting up and beginning to
pace the room again, trying not to look at the bed behind the
screen. 'What on earth's the matter with me? It isn't as if it's the
first time – and yet . . . Anyway, what was it about her that was
so special, and what actually happened? It *was* like a kind of
sunstroke! And above all, what can I possibly do with myself all
day in this backwater, without her?'

He still remembered the whole of her, down to the last tiny

detail, remembered the smell of her tanned skin and her cotton dress, her strong body and the lively, easy, gay sound of her voice . . . The sensation left behind by the pleasures all her feminine perfections had so recently afforded him was still extraordinarily alive inside him, but now somehow there was a second, completely new feeling – a mysterious, incomprehensible feeling which hadn't existed during their time together, which he couldn't possibly have divined within himself the previous day when he was embarking upon what was to be, he believed, merely an amusing friendship, and which now there was no longer any chance of explaining to her. 'The main thing is,' he thought, 'that now I'll never be able to tell her! And what am I going to do, how am I going to live through this interminable day with these memories and this incurable torment, in this godforsaken little town above that same shimmering Volga which carried her away aboard her pink steamer?'

He had to find refuge, find something to do, something to distract him, somewhere to go. Resolutely he put on his cap, took up his riding-crop and having walked rapidly, jingling his spurs, along the empty corridor, ran down the steep staircase to the hotel entrance . . . Ah, but where was he to go? A cab stood at the door and the young driver, dressed in a sleek, sleeveless tunic, sat quietly smoking a small cigar. Lost and bewildered, the lieutenant glanced at him: how could he sit there on his box, smoking peacefully like that, and how could anyone be so utterly unremarkable and unconcerned and indifferent? 'I must be the only one in the whole town to be so desperately unhappy,' he told himself as he made his way to the market-place.

The market was already packing up. For some reason he wandered for a time over the fresh dung which lay between the carts and wagons loaded with cucumbers, picking his way through brand-new bowls and jugs, and peasantwomen sitting on the ground called out to him, shouting each other down, and lifting their pots in their hands tapped them with their fingers to make them ring out in demonstration of their quality, while their men-folk deafened him, bellowing: 'Prime cucumbers! Buy my cucumbers, your Honour!' All this was so silly and absurd that he fled from the market-place. He went to the church where the singing, in recognition of a duty fulfilled, was already loud, merry and determined, and then trudged round and round a small, scorching, neglected garden clinging to the side of a hill above the infinite, steely-pale breadth of the river. The straps and buttons on his tunic had become so hot that he could no longer touch them. The band inside his cap was sodden with sweat and his face scarlet . . . Returning to the hotel, he entered with pleasure the big cool deserted dining-room on the ground floor, with pleasure removed his cap, sat down at a little table beside an open window which admitted some breeze with the gusts of heat, and ordered cold soup with ice-cubes . . . All was well, in everything there was an immense happiness, a great joy! Even the blazing heat and all the smells of the market-place, the whole unfamiliar little town and the old, provincial hotel contained this joy, and yet at the same time his heart was simply being torn apart. He downed several glasses of vodka, taking little bites of dill-pickled cucumber, and felt that, without a second thought, he would be glad to die the next day if by some miracle she could be brought back so that they could spend one more day, this day, together – spend it together in order that, *only* in order that, he might tell her, prove to her, convince her in some way, how painfully and rapturously he loved her . . . Why prove it? Why convince her? He didn't know why, but it was more necessary than life itself.

'My nerves are shot to pieces,' he said, pouring himself a fifth glass of vodka.

He pushed his soup bowl away, asked for black coffee, and lighting a cigarette tried to collect his thoughts. What was to be done now? How was he to rid himself of this sudden, unexpected love? But ridding himself of it, he felt only too vividly, was impossible. He leapt to his feet once more, took his riding-crop, and having asked the way to the post office, hurried off in that direction, the words of a telegram prepared in his head: 'Henceforth my entire life, forever until the grave, is yours, it is in your hands.' But having reached the stout-walled old building which housed the post and telegraph offices he stopped aghast: he knew the town where she lived and that she had a husband and a three-year-old daughter, but was totally ignorant of both her Christian name and surname. He had asked her to tell him several times at dinner the evening before, and again in the hotel, but on each occasion she had merely laughed and answered:

'Why do you need to know who I am or what my name is?'

On the corner near the post office was the window of a photographer's studio. He spent a long time contemplating a large portrait of some military gentleman in thick epaulettes, with bulging eyes, a shallow brow, astonishingly magnificent sideburns and a hugely broad chest completely covered in medals. How absurd and frightening the humdrum and usual is when the heart has been vanquished – yes, vanquished, he now knew it to be so – by this terrifying sunstroke, by too great a love, too great a joy! He glanced at a pair of newly-weds – a young man in white tie and tails, with close-shaven head, standing at attention with a girl in bridal tulle on his arm – and shifted his gaze to the picture of a pretty, pert young woman wearing her student's cap at a rakish angle . . . Then, plunged into an agonizing envy of all these unknown, happy and unafflicted persons, he began to stare intently down the street.

'Where shall I go? What shall I do?'

The street was completely deserted. All the houses were white, two-storeyed merchants' dwellings with large gardens, and it seemed as if not a soul lived in them; thick white dust lay on the carriageway and everything was blinding, everything bathed in burning, fiery, joyous, but somehow pointless sunlight. In the distance the street climbed upwards, arching its humped back against the cloudless, faintly grey skyline which cast its reflection below. There was a hint of the south about it all which reminded him of Sebastopol, Kerch and Anapa. He found this particularly unbearable. And head lowered, eyes narrowed against the glare, gazing down in concentration at his feet and staggering from side to side, stumbling as his spurs caught against each other, the lieutenant turned back his steps.

He arrived at the hotel so overcome by exhaustion that he might have been returning from some epic march in Turkestan or the Sahara. Gathering the last of his strength, he went to his big empty room. The room had already been tidied and cleared of the last vestiges of her presence – only a single hairpin, which she had overlooked, lay on the bedside table. He took off his tunic and glanced at himself in the mirror: his face – a typical officer's face grey from its tan, blond moustache bleached further by the sun, bluish whites of eyes appearing whiter still against the tanned skin – now held an agitated, deranged expression, whilst in the fine white shirt with its high starched little collar there was something youthful and deeply sad. He lay down on his back on the bed, dangling his dusty boots over the edge. The windows were open and the curtains drawn, and now and again a soft little breeze would fill them as it came wafting in laden with the heat blowing off blazing tin roofs and with all that luminous world, silent now and deserted, beside the Volga. Hands folded behind his head, he lay staring fixedly in front of him. Then, clenching his teeth, he lowered his eyelids, feeling the tears roll down his cheeks – and at last fell asleep. When he opened his eyes again the evening sun was glowing red and yellow behind the curtains. The breeze had died away and the room felt stuffy and dry as an oven . . . Remembering both the day before and the morning that had just passed, it seemed to him as if it had all been ten years earlier.

Unhurriedly he rose, unhurriedly washed his face, parted the curtains and rang for the samovar and his bill, and then sat for a long time sipping lemon tea. Later he ordered a cab and had his luggage brought downstairs, and as he climbed onto the cab's rusty discoloured upholstery, gave the porter five whole roubles.

'Seems like it was us brought you here last night, your Honour!' the driver said cheerfully, picking up the reins.

By the time they had driven down to the jetty a dark blue night had descended upon the Volga and many tiny coloured lights were already sprinkled along the river, while bigger lights swung from the masts of an approaching steamer.

'Timed it just right!' said the cabby ingratiatingly.

The lieutenant gave him five roubles as well, bought a ticket and went out onto the landing-stage . . . Exactly as on the day before, there was a dull thud against the mooring and a slight giddiness from the unsteady rocking underfoot, then the flying rope and the noise of water boiling and surging forward under the paddles as the ship went into reverse for a moment . . . And he found the crowded steamer extraordinarily welcoming and agreeable with all of her lights ablaze and a smell of cooking in the air.

In a moment they set off again upstream, in the direction in which she too had been carried away only that morning.

Far ahead, the dark summer twilight had faded, its myriad dusky colours reflected drowsily in the river which here and there still gleamed in trembling, distant ripples beneath it, and the lights scattered throughout the surrounding darkness drifted further and further back.

The lieutenant sat under an awning on the deck, feeling that he had aged ten years.

Alpes Maritimes, 1925

The Caucasus

Translated by Sophie Lund

On arrival in Moscow I took rooms, furtively, in an obscure
lodging house tucked away in an alley close to the Arbat, and
lived the tedious existence of a recluse – from one meeting with
her to the next. She came to me on only three occasions during
that period, and each time arrived in haste, exclaiming:

'I can only stay a minute . . .'

She was pale, with the exquisite pallor of a woman filled with
love and apprehension, her voice kept breaking, and the way in
which, having cast down her umbrella without caring where it
fell, she hastened to lift her veil in order to embrace me,
overwhelmed me with rapture and pity.

'It seems to me,' she said, 'that he suspects something, maybe
knows something. Perhaps he's read one of your letters, or found
a key to fit my desk . . . I think, with his harsh proud nature, he's
capable of anything. Once he told me, point-blank: "I'll stop at
nothing to defend my honour, the honour of an officer and a
husband." Now, for some reason, he literally watches my every
move, and if our plan is to succeed I must be extremely
careful . . . He's already agreed to let me go because I've
convinced him that I'll die unless I get a glimpse of the south and
the sea, but in the name of God be patient!'

Our plan was audacious: to leave by the same train for the
Caucasian coast, and to live there in some totally wild spot for
three or four weeks. I knew that coastline, I'd stayed at one time
near Sochi – young and lonely – and for the rest of my life would
remember those autumn evenings amid the dark cypresses, close

to the cold grey waves. Her face grew white when I said: 'And now I'll be there with you in the mountain jungles, beside the tropical sea . . .' We didn't believe in the realization of our plan until the very last minute – to us it seemed too great a happiness.

In Moscow, cold rain was falling, summer seemed to have gone away, never to return – it was dirty, gloomy, the streets shone, black and wet, with the open umbrellas of passers-by and the raised hoods of hansoms quivering in motion. And it was a dark filthy night when I drove to the station, everything inside me numb with cold and dread. I ran through the station and along the platform, with my hat pulled down over my eyes and my face hidden in the collar of my overcoat.

The small first-class compartment I had reserved in advance was filled with the sound of rain drumming upon its roof. Hastily I drew the little curtain, and when the porter, wiping a wet hand on his white apron, had taken his tip and gone away, I turned the key in the door. Then, parting the curtain very slightly, I stood transfixed at the window, eyes fastened upon the motley crowd of people scurrying up and down beside the carriage with their luggage in the dim glare of the station lamps. We had agreed that I would come to the station as early as possible and she as late as possible, so as to avoid any chance of my bumping into either of them on the platform. Now, they should have already arrived. I stared out with ever-increasing intensity – still they didn't come. The bell rang for the second time – I went cold with fear: she had missed the train or at the last minute he had refused to let her go! But suddenly, at the very next instant, I was stunned by the sight of his tall figure, the officer's cap, the narrow tunic, the suede-gloved hand with which he held her arm as he strode along. I started back from the window and fell into a corner of the banquette. Next door there was a second-class compartment. In my mind's eye I saw him enter beside her proprietorially, look round – had the porter installed her to his satisfaction? – take off his glove and his cap, kiss her, and make the sign of the cross over her . . . The third bell deafened me, the first movement of the train plunged me into a stupor . . . The train gathered momentum, weaving and swaying from side to side, and then, at full steam, settled to an even speed . . . With a hand cold as ice I thrust a ten-rouble note at the guard who brought her to me and transferred her luggage.

When she came in she didn't even kiss me, but just gave a pitiful little smile, and sitting down on the banquette removed her hat, disentangling it from her hair.

'I couldn't eat any dinner,' she said. 'I thought I'd never be able to see this appalling role through. And I'm dreadfully thirsty. Give me some mineral water.' She used the intimate singular for the first time. 'I'm convinced he'll come after me. I gave him two addresses, Gelendzhik and Gagry. So there we are, three or four days and he'll be in Gelendzhik . . . Well, let him, I'd prefer death to suffering like this . . .'

In the morning, when I went out into the corridor, it was sunny and close; a smell of soap, eau de cologne, and everything that perfumes a crowded railway carriage early in the day, came from the wash-rooms. Beyond the warm windows, murky with dust, lay flat scorched steppe, wide dusty roads could be seen and carts pulled by bullocks, signal boxes flashed past with the canary-yellow discs of sunflowers and scarlet mallow in their front gardens . . . Then came an endless expanse of bare plain with tumuli and burial grounds, unbearable dry sunlight, sky like a dustladen cloud, and eventually the first ghostly traces of mountains on the horizon . . .

She sent him a postcard from Gelendzhik and another from Gagry. She wrote that she was still unsure where she would be staying.

Then we followed the coastline south.

We found a primitive spot overgrown with forests of plane trees, flowering shrubs, mahogany, magnolias and pomegranates, with feathery palms and dark cypresses rising among them.

I would awaken early, and while she was still asleep, before tea which we took at seven o'clock, walk across low hills deep into the woods. The hot sun would already be strong, clear and joyous. In the forest, a fragrant mist, gleaming and pale-blue, parted and melted away, beyond the distant leafy heights snow-capped mountains shone with a whiteness old as time . . . On my way back I would pass through the village bazaar shimmering in the heat, filled with the scent of pressed dung burning in its chimneys: it seethed with commerce and you could hardly move in the crush of people, horses and donkeys – a host of tribesmen from various hill tribes congregated in the bazaar every morning – while Circassian women walked with their gliding step in floor-length robes and crimson slippers, their heads swathed in black, darting occasional bird-like glances from within their funereal wrappings.

Afterwards we'd go to the beach which was always completely deserted, and swim and sunbathe until it was time for lunch. After lunch – invariably fish grilled on a skewer, white wine, nuts and fruit – in the sultry twilight of our hut under its tiled roof, hot merry shafts of light filtered through the shutters.

When the heat had abated and we threw open the window, that part of the sea which we were able to glimpse from it, through the cypress trees growing on the slope below us, was the colour of violets, and lay so smooth, so peaceful, that it seemed as if there would never be an end to this tranquillity and beauty.

At sunset, extraordinary clouds often gathered above the sea; they blazed with such splendour that from time to time she would lie down on the ottoman, cover her face with a gauze scarf, and begin to weep; another two or three weeks and once more – Moscow!

The nights were warm and impenetrable, in the black darkness fireflies swam, glinted and shone with a topaz light, tree frogs croaked with the sound of glass bells. When the eye became accustomed to the darkness, stars and the crests of mountains appeared on high, trees we hadn't noticed in daylight were etched above the village. And the whole night long, from the direction of the inn, came the dull beat of a drum and the throaty, mournful, despairingly ecstatic wail of what seemed to be the same single, endless song.

Not far from us, in a gulley close to the shore, running from the forest to the sea, a small transparent river leapt in its stony bed. How exquisitely its brilliance seethed and splintered, in that magic hour when, from beyond the mountains and the forests, like some miraculous being, the late moon peered intently down!

At night sometimes, menacing clouds massed from the direction of the mountains and a malevolent storm raged, again and again in the clamorous graveyard blackness of the forest enchanted leafy pits yawned wide, and the heavens high above were riven by primeval claps of thunder. Then in the forest eaglets awoke and mewed, a snow leopard roared and jackals yelped . . . Once a whole pack of them came to our lighted window – they always run to a habitation on nights like these – and we opened the window and looked down upon them as they stood under the glittering downpour yelping to be let in . . . Gazing at them, she wept with joy.

He searched for her in Gelendzhik, in Gagry and in Sochi. On the morning after his arrival in Sochi he swam in the sea, then shaved, put on a clean shirt and a snow-white high-collared tunic, lunched at his hotel on the terrace of the restaurant, drank a bottle of champagne, took coffee with chartreuse, and smoked a leisurely cigar. Returning to his room, he lay down on the divan and using two revolvers shot himself through both temples.

12 November 1937

Late Hour

Translated by David Richards

What a long time since I was last there, I said to myself. Not since I was nineteen. I used to live in Russia, I felt it was my country, I enjoyed complete freedom to go where I pleased and a journey of three hundred versts was no great trouble. But I still hadn't gone there, I'd kept putting it off. And the years unfolded and passed – and the decades. But now it mustn't be put off any longer; it was now or never. I must take advantage of this last and only chance, since the hour was late and I wouldn't meet anyone.

So I crossed over the river by the bridge, with everything all round clearly visible in the moonlight of a July night.

The bridge was as familiar and unchanged as if I'd seen it yesterday – crudely ancient, humped and somehow not made of stone but rather petrified by time into a state of eternal indestructibility. As a schoolboy I used to think it had been there in Batu's day. However, the town's antiquity was reflected only in a few surviving fragments of the old walls on the precipice above the cathedral and in this bridge. All the rest was merely old and provincial, nothing more. There was one strange thing though, one thing which indicated that nevertheless something had changed on earth since I was a boy, or a youth: formerly the river had not been navigable, but now it had obviously been deepened and dredged. The moon was to my left, high above the river, and in its vacillating light and the twinkling, trembling brightness of the water lay a white paddle-steamer which seemed to be empty, so silent was it, although all its port-holes were illuminated like fixed golden eyes, each one reflected on the water in a golden column of light. The steamer appeared to be standing on them. It had been like that in Yaroslavl, on the Suez Canal, and on the Nile. In Paris the nights are damp and dark and a misty pink glow illumines the pitch-dark sky; the Seine flows under the bridges like black tar, but columns of light also hang down from the lamp-posts on the bridges – only there they are tri-coloured, white, blue and red, like Russian national flags. Here the bridge had no lamp-posts and was dry and dusty. Ahead of me, uphill, were the dark gardens of the town, and above the gardens loomed the fire watch-tower. My God, how indescribably happy I had been! It was during a fire one night that I first kissed your hand, and you squeezed mine in response – I shall never forget that covert consent of yours. The whole street was dark with people in the sinister, extraordinary light. I was staying at your house when the alarm sounded and everyone rushed to the windows and then out of the gate. The fire was in the distance, on the other side of the river, but it was burning terribly brightly, greedily, and fast. Like a blackish-purple fleece, thick clouds of smoke were piling up, and out of them huge red sheets of flame shot high into the air; close to us they threw copper ripples onto the dome of St Michael the Archangel's. And in the close-packed crowd, amid the anxious, half-sympathetic, half-excited murmur of the people who had gathered from all parts of the town, I caught the scent of your virginal hair, neck and gingham dress – and suddenly I plucked up my courage and, in trepidation, took your hand . . .

Over the bridge I walked uphill and entered the town by a paved road.

In the town there was not a single light anywhere and no living soul. All was quiet and spacious, calm and sad – with the sadness of a Russian town asleep in the steppes at night. In one or two of the gardens the leaves on the trees were cautiously rustling, just audibly, in the steady current of a gentle July breeze which came from the open countryside and blew softly in my face. I walked along with the full moon accompanying me, bowling its mirror-roundness through the darkness of the branches. The broad streets lay in shadow; only in the houses on the right, which the shadow did not reach, were the white walls illuminated, while the black window-panes radiated a sable gloss; and I walked in the shadows, stepping along the dappled pavement which seemed to be strewn with a black silky lace. She'd had an evening dress like that, very elegant, long and close-fitting. It suited her slender figure and dark young eyes extraordinarily well. When she wore it she had been mysterious and woundingly oblivious of my presence. Where had that been? At whose house?

I aimed to spend a little time in Old Street. I could have reached it by another, shorter route, but I turned into these wide streets and gardens because I wanted to take a look at the school. And when I reached it I was again astonished: here too everything remained as it had been half a century before – there was the stone wall, the stone yard and the big stone building in the yard, all just as banal and boring as they had been in my day. I lingered at the gate and tried to summon up the sadness and compassion of memories, but failed. Yes, a close-cropped first-former in a new blue cap with a badge of little silver palms over the peak and a new uniform greatcoat with silver buttons used to go in at those gates, then later a slim youth in a grey jacket and foppish trousers with bootstraps – but was that me?

Old Street struck me only as being a little narrower than it used to seem. Everything else was unchanged: the pot-holed roadway, not a single tree, the dusty merchants' houses on both sides, and the pavements which were also so full of potholes that it was better to walk in the middle of the road in the full light of the moon . . . And the night was almost the same as that earlier one. Only then it had been at the end of August, when the whole town used to smell of the apples lying in heaps in the markets and it was so hot that it was a pleasure to go about in just a Russian shirt and Cossack belt . . . Can you remember that night where you are now, perhaps in heaven?

I still couldn't make up my mind to go as far as your house. It wouldn't have changed either, I supposed; for that very reason seeing it would be more frightening. New people, strangers, must be living there now. Your father, your mother and your brother all outlived you, my young love, but their time came and they also died. And all my people had died, not only relations, but also many, many others together with whom, as friends or acquaintances, I began my life; how long ago it was that they too began life, confident that it would never end, but everything began, unfolded and reached its close before my eyes, so rapidly and before my eyes! And I sat on a kerbstone beside one of the merchants' houses, inaccessible behind its locks and gates, and began to think about what she had been like in those distant times which we shared: the plainly-styled dark hair, the clear eyes, the lightly tanned, youthful face and the light summer dress over a chaste, firm, free young body . . . That was the beginning of our love, a time of still unclouded happiness, closeness, trust, rapturous tenderness and joy . . .

There is something very special about the warm light nights of Russian provincial towns in late summer. What peace, what a sense of well-being! An old man with a rattle wanders round the happy nocturnal town, but only for his own pleasure since there's nothing to watch for. Sleep peacefully, good people, you are watched over by God's favour, by that high shining sky which the old man glances up at as he wanders along the roadway still warm from the day, and only occasionally, for amusement, launches his rattle into a dancing trill. And yes, it was on such a night, at the same late hour, when he was the only one in the town not sleeping, that you waited for me in your already parched late-summer garden and I slipped secretly into it. I quietly opened the wicket gate which you'd earlier left unlocked, quietly and quickly ran across the yard, and on the other side of the barn at the end of the yard I entered the motley twilight of the garden where your dress showed faintly white in the distance on a bench under the apple trees, and quickly coming up to you, with a joyous start I suddenly met the gleam of your waiting eyes.

And we sat and sat in a stupor of happiness. With one arm I embraced you, feeling your heart beat; my other hand held yours, and through it I sensed your whole being. And it was so late that even the rattle was not to be heard – the old man had lain down somewhere on a bench with his pipe between his teeth, warming himself in the moonlight. If I looked to the right I saw the moon shining high and sinless over the yard and the roof of the house radiating a scaly glitter. If I looked to the left I saw a path overgrown with dried-up grass disappearing under yet more apple trees, and beyond them, peeping out low over another garden, a solitary green star, which twinkled impassively, yet also expectantly, delivering a soundless message. But I saw both the yard and the star only fleetingly: there was only one thing in the world – the twilight and the radiant gleam of your eyes in the twilight.

And then you accompanied me to the wicket-gate, and I said:

'If there's a future life and we meet in it, I will kneel down there and kiss your feet for everything you've given me on earth.'

I went out into the middle of the bright street and set off back to my inn. Looking back, I saw a patch of white still at the wicket-gate.

Now, getting up from the kerbstone, I went back the same way that I'd come: apart from Old Street, I had another aim, which I was frightened to own to, but which I knew I had to accomplish. So I set off – to have just a quick look and then go away for ever.

The path was again familiar. Straight on, then left across the market, and from the market along Monastery Street to the exit from the town.

The market is like a town within the town. The rows have a very strong smell. In the refreshment stall it is very dark under the awnings which stretch over the long tables and benches. In the hardware row a rusty-framed icon of a large-eyed Saviour hangs on a chain above the middle of the passageway. In the bakers' row a whole flock of pigeons would always be running about in the morning, pecking at the roadway. On the way to school there would be so many of them! And all of them fat, with rainbow-coloured crops, pecking and running about, waddling in a feminine, provocative manner, rocking from side to side and rhythmically jerking their heads as though not noticing you; they'd fly up, with whistling wings, only after you'd almost stepped on one of them. And at night big black rats would run quickly and busily about, repulsive and frightening.

Monastery Street is an escape into the countryside – for some a road home out of the town into the country, for others a road to the city of the dead. In Paris, house number so-and-so in such-and-such street will be distinguished for forty-eight hours from all the other houses by the theatrically plague-stricken appearance of its doorway which will be framed in black and silver mourning; for forty-eight hours a black-edged sheet of paper lies on a funereally draped little table in the porch, and polite visitors sign their names as a mark of condolence; then at some final appointed moment a huge carriage with a black canopy stops at the porch, its woodwork pitch-black, like a plague coffin, the carved round edges of the canopy testifying to heaven with their huge white stars, and the corners of the roof are decorated with ornate black plumes, ostrich-feathers from the underworld; the carriage is drawn by strapping beasts in coal-black, spiked horse-cloths with round white eyelets; immensely high up on the box, waiting for the corpse to be brought out, sits an old drunkard, also symbolically attired in a stage funeral coat and tricorn and doubtless inwardly smirking over those solemn words: *Requiem aeternam dona eis, Domine, et lux perpetua luceat eis* . . . Here everything is different. A breeze wafts down Monastery Street from the countryside, and into that breeze the open coffin is carried on linen cloths, the rice-coloured face with the bright wreath on its forehead above the closed convex eyelids swaying from side to side. That was how she too must have been carried.

At the exit from the town, to the left of the highway, stands the monastery built in the time of Tsar Aleksey Mikhaylovich, with its ever-shut fortress-like gates and its fortress-like walls, behind which gleam the gilded turnip-shaped domes of the church. Further out, in the open countryside, is a vast square of more, low walls: they enclose a spacious grove, divided by long intersecting avenues alongside which, under the old elms, limes and birches, stand a variety of crosses and memorials. There the gates were ajar, and I suddenly saw the main avenue, smooth and endless. I timidly took off my hat and went in. How late it was, and how silent! The moon already hung low behind the trees, but everything round me, as far as the eye could reach, was still clearly visible. The entire expanse of this grove of the dead with its crosses and memorials showed up in a clear pattern in the transparent shadows. The wind had died down for the hour before dawn and the light and dark patches which still stood out under the trees were motionless. Suddenly at the far end of the grove, behind the cemetery church, I saw something move and come rushing towards me at furious speed like a dark ball – terrified, I jumped aside, my whole head turning ice-cold and numb while my heart lurched and missed a beat . . . What was it? It rushed on and disappeared. But the heart in my breast remained still. And so with that stilled heart which I bore within me like a heavy chalice, I went on. I knew where I had to go and walked straight down the avenue, and at the very end of it, only a few paces from the back wall, I stopped. In front of me, on level ground in the dry grass, lay a solitary, long, rather narrow stone, with its head towards the wall. And beyond the wall, like a marvellous gem, hung a low green star, radiant like that former one, but mute and still.

19 October 1938

Visiting Cards

Translated by Sophie Lund

It was the beginning of autumn and the steamer *Goncharov* was
making her way along the deserted reaches of the Volga. The first
cold weather had arrived, and a chill wind blew brisk and sharp
in her direction from the eastern, already rust-coloured shore,
across the grey gulfs of the river's Asiatic wastes, whipping the
flag at her stern and the hats, caps and clothes of those who
walked her decks, creasing their faces and filling their sleeves and
skirts. Aimlessly and monotonously, a lone seagull followed the
steamer – now flying close behind her stern, banking steeply on
pointed wings, now slipping away to the side, slanting into the
distance as if it didn't know what to do with itself in this great
wilderness of river and grey autumnal sky.

And there was almost no-one on board: only a team of peasants
on the lower deck and a mere three people, walking up and down
passing and re-passing each other, on the upper one: two
second-class passengers, bound for the same destination and
inseparable as they paced the deck invariably side-by-side and
deep in some business-like discussion, very alike in their anony-
mous appearance, and one first-class, a man of thirty or so, a
writer who had been recently acclaimed, distinguished by an air of
melancholy or perhaps angry seriousness, and to some extent by
his physique. He was tall and powerfully built, a little stooping in
the manner of some strong people, well dressed and in his own
way handsome: with his dark brown hair, he belonged to that
eastern Russian type which crops up now and then in Moscow
among her ancient merchant population; and he had indeed

emerged from that breed although he no longer had anything in common with it.

He walked with a firm step, a solitary figure in stout expensive shoes, black Cheviot cloth overcoat and checked English tweed cap, striding to and fro into the wind and with his back to it, breathing in the autumn and that potent Volga air. Walking up to the stern, he would stop and stand gazing at the expanding grey swell of the river racing along in the wake of the steamer and then, turning abruptly, walk to the bows, into the wind, ducking his head with its ballooning tweed cap and listening to the measured thud of the paddles from which streams of rushing water fell in glassy sheets. At last he suddenly paused and gave a sombre smile. Rising out of the well of the staircase leading from the lower deck, from the third class, was an inexpensive little hat and under it the pinched, charming face of the woman he had become acquainted with quite by chance the evening before. Taking long strides, he went to meet her. Having emerged onto the deck, she too, with an answering smile, made her unsteady way towards him, bowled along by the wind which blew her sideways and holding on to her hat with a thin hand, dressed in a skimpy little coat that revealed the slender legs beneath it.

'How did you sleep?' he asked in a loud masculine voice as he approached.

'Perfectly,' she answered with exaggerated gaiety. 'I always sleep like a log . . .'

He took her hand in his large one and glanced into her eyes. She made a joyful effort and met his gaze.

'What made you sleep so long, my angel?' he asked with familiarity. 'All self-respecting folk are already at lunch.'

'I couldn't stop dreaming,' she replied in an animated way quite out of keeping with everything about her appearance.

'What about?'

'Never you mind!'

'Oh, take care! "That's how little children drown on a summer's day. The Chechen walks beyond the river and far, far away."'

'Well, it's your Chechen I'm waiting for!' she answered with the same cheerful animation.

'We'd do far better to go and find a glass of vodka and a bowl of soup,' he said, thinking she probably couldn't even afford lunch.

She stamped her feet flirtatiously.

'Yes, yes, vodka! It's damned cold!'

And they walked rapidly to the first-class dining-room, she leading the way, he following behind, eyeing her already a little greedily.

He had thought about her the previous night. Yesterday, after he had met her accidentally at the steamer's rail and drawn her into conversation as the ship slid through the dusk towards some steep black shore where there was already a scattering of lights, they had sat together on deck, on the long bench which ran parallel to the row of first-class cabins beneath the white translucent blinds at their windows, but he hadn't lingered – something which later that night he had come to regret. To his surprise he discovered during the night that he already wanted her. Why? Could it just be in response to the customary lure of unknown travelling companions? Now, sitting beside her in the dining-room, clinking glasses over chilled caviare and hot white bread, he knew why he found her so desirable, and waited impatiently for the affair to reach its conclusion. Because it was all – the vodka, her free and easy manner – such an extraordinary contrast to the way she looked, the excitement he felt inside grew fiercer all the time.

'One more glass each and we'll have an orgy on our hands,' he said.

'Yes,' she replied in the same vein. 'An orgy. But what wonderful vodka!'

Of course he found her touching because the day before she had become so flustered when he mentioned his name, so amazed at this unforeseen encounter with a famous author – to sense and witness this confusion was as always most agreeable: it always enhances a woman, as long as she is not hopelessly plain and dull-witted, and fosters a certain intimacy between you, imparting a degree of boldness to your approach and already giving you a kind of right over her. However, this was not all that had aroused him: it looked as if in addition he had impressed her purely as a man, while she had moved him by her poverty and artlessness. He had perfected a familiar manner towards his women admirers, a swift and easy progression from the first moment of meeting to an informal, supposedly artistic attitude and a deliberately casual way of asking questions: Who are you? Where are you from? Are you married? That was how he had interrogated her the previous night, peering through the evening shadows at the multi-coloured lights of the buoys casting long reflections upon the darkening water round the steamer, and at the red glow of the wood-fires burning on the rafts, sniffing the gentle smoke which came drifting across from them and thinking: I must remember this – at this moment there's a hint of fish soup in the smell of that smoke.

He'd asked her: 'May I know your name?'

She had quickly told him her name and patronymic.

'Are you on your way home from somewhere?'

'I've been to see my sister in Sviyazhsk. Her husband died suddenly, you see, leaving her in a dreadful state . . .'

At first she had been so ill-at-ease that she kept staring into the distance. After a while her replies became a little bolder.

'And are you married too?'

She gave a strange little laugh.

'Yes, and not for the first year, alas . . .'

'Why alas?'

'I leapt into marriage, stupidly, far too young. There's hardly time to look round before life is over.'

'Surely there's still a long way to go.'

'Alas, not really. And I've experienced absolutely nothing of life.'

'It's not too late to begin. You could try.'

At this point she shook her head with a sudden humorous gesture:

'I will then!'

'What is your husband? A civil servant?'

She waved her hand.

'Oh, a very nice and kind but unfortunately totally uninteresting man. The secretary of our local district council.'

'How adorable and how unhappy she is,' he'd thought, taking out his cigarette case.

'Would you like a cigarette?'

'Yes, very much.'

Then clumsily but courageously she had begun to smoke, taking rapid feminine little puffs. And once again he'd felt a tremor of pity go through him, for her and her lack of restraint, and together with that pity had come a wave of tenderness and a voluptuous longing to take advantage of her naïvety and belated inexperience, which he could already tell would lead to extreme daring. Now sitting in the dining-room he looked impatiently at her thin hands and the faded and thus even more poignant little face and the wealth of carelessly pinned hair which, once she had removed her black hat and allowed her little grey coat to slip off the shoulders of a cheap cotton frock, she kept tossing back. He was excited and touched by the candour with which, the evening before, she had spoken of her married life and of no longer being young, and the way in which, having suddenly taken her courage in both hands, she was beginning to talk and act in a manner that was so extraordinarily unbecoming to her. She was slightly flushed from the vodka, her pale lips had even turned a little pink, and her eyes were filled with a sleepily teasing light.

'You know,' she said suddenly. 'We were talking about our dreams. Shall I tell you what I dreamed of most when I was a

schoolgirl? Of having some visiting cards printed. We'd become
poor as church mice in those days, and sold the last of our estate
and moved into town, so there was absolutely no-one I could have
given them to, but oh, how I dreamed. Terribly silly . . .'

His jaw tightened and he gripped her little hand, feeling every
one of the tiny bones under its delicate skin, but she, misunder-
standing completely, carried it to his lips herself like an accom-
plished seductress and cast him a languorous glance.

'Let's go to my cabin.'

'Yes, let's . . . It's a little stuffy in here, so full of smoke.'
And shaking back her hair, she picked up her hat.

In the corridor he put his arms around her. Proudly, volup-
tuously, she looked back at him over her shoulder, and in the
hatred of love and desire he almost bit her cheek. She offered him
her lips like a bacchante, again over her shoulder.

In the half-light of the cabin with its slatted grill over the
window, hurrying to please him and make the fullest, most
reckless use of the happiness that had fallen to her lot in the
company of this handsome, strong and famous man, she im-
mediately unbuttoned her dress, treading her way out of it as it
fell to the floor to emerge slender as a boy in a thin little chemise
and white drawers, her arms and shoulders bare – and he felt an
agonizing pang at the innocence of it all.

'Shall I take everything off?' she asked him, whispering just
like a little girl.

'Yes, everything,' he replied, his mood darkening by the
minute.

Quickly and submissively, she stepped out of the pile of
underclothes thrown on the floor and stood completely naked
save for cheap grey stockings held up by plain garters and a pair
of cheap little black slippers, her pale lavender-grey body turning
taut and cool in that way peculiar to female flesh when shivering
with nerves and covered in goose pimples. Giving him a tipsy,
triumphant look she took hold of her hair and began to unpin it.

He grew cold as he watched her. In fact, her body revealed itself as better and younger than he could have anticipated. The thin collar-bones and rib-cage stood out, in keeping with the thin face and slender shins. Yet the hips were even large. Her belly with its small deep navel was hollow and the swelling triangle of beautiful dark hair below it matched the abundance of dark hair on her head which, when she had removed the last pin, tumbled in thick strands down her thin back with its prominent vertebrae. She bent forward to catch her stockings before they fell around her ankles, and her small breasts with their cold, wrinkled brown nipples hung like two emaciated little pears – exquisite in their poverty. And he forced her to experience that ultimate shamelessness which, because it suited her so ill, aroused him to such heights of tenderness, pity and desire . . .

Through the slats of the blind, jutting up at a sharp angle, nothing could be seen, but she stared at them out of the corner of her eye in an ecstasy of terror, listening to the footsteps and the carefree chatter of the passengers walking on the deck immediately below their window, and that increased still further the rapture of her depravity: how near they were, talking and strolling by, and it didn't even enter their heads to wonder what might be taking place a mere step away in that white cabin!

Afterwards he laid her on the bunk, as if she were no longer alive. Teeth clenched, she lay with her eyes closed and already with a look of sorrowful peace on her white, utterly young face.

Just before evening, when the steamer tied up at the place where she was to disembark, she stood quietly by his side, eyelashes lowered. He kissed her cold little hand with that love which stays somewhere in the heart for the rest of one's life, and she, without looking back, ran down the gangway into the rough crowd on the quayside.

5 October 1940

Zoyka and Valeria

Translated by Sophie Lund

During the winter Levitsky had been spending all his spare time in the Danilevskys' Moscow apartment, then when summer came he began to visit them at their dacha in the pine forests lining the Kazan road.

He was twenty-four years old and in the fifth year of his course, but when he was with the Danilevskys only the doctor called him 'colleague' – to everyone else he was George or Georgik. Because of his lonely and impressionable nature he was constantly attaching himself to one or other of the households of his acquaintance, quickly becoming one of the family and frequenting the house day after day, even from morning to night if his studies permitted – and now he'd attached himself to the Danilevskys. Here too, not only the lady of the house but even the children – the exceedingly plump Zoyka and big-eared Grishka – treated him as if he were some distant, homeless relative. His manner was unassuming and kind-hearted, helpful and uncommunicative, although he was always very ready to respond to any remark addressed to him.

Danilevsky's patients were received by an elderly woman in a nurse's uniform. They passed into a spacious lobby strewn with rugs and filled with massive antique furniture where, putting on her spectacles, the woman would gaze sternly into her appointments book and, pencil in hand, either assign them some future date or lead them through tall doors into the waiting-room where they would have to remain for ages until, having been summoned into an adjoining office, they were interrogated and examined by a young assistant in a sugar-white coat: only after that would they be admitted to Danilevsky himself in his big consulting-room where, standing along the back wall, there was a large couch upon which some of them would be required to lie and stretch out in the most abject and nervously awkward postures. Everything filled the patients with unease – not only the assistant and the woman in the lobby, where the shining copper disk of the pendulum in the antique grandfather clock swung back and forth with funereal deliberation, but the whole solemn propriety of the opulent, spacious apartment and the expectant hush of the waiting-room where no-one dared breathe a superfluous sigh and everyone was conscious of having come to some very special, eternally lifeless place where even Danilevsky himself – tall, solid and a little coarse – hardly smiled as much as once a year. But they were mistaken: in the private areas of the apartment beyond the double doors to the right of the entrance hall, there would almost invariably be the hubbub of guests, the samovar would never leave the dining-room table, the parlour maid rushed to and fro carrying now extra cups and glasses, now jars filled with preserves, now buns and biscuits, and Danilevsky, even in consulting hours, would often quickly tiptoe across the hall and while the patients waited, convinced that he must be terribly busy with some desperately ill person, sit down, sip tea and say of them to the assembled company:

'They can damn well wait a moment or two, blast them!'

One day as he was sitting there like this, and with a teasing smile contemplating Levitsky's narrow, skinny, slightly stooped body, slightly bandy legs and hollow stomach, his freckled face with its taut delicate skin, eyes like those of a bird of prey and tightly curling red hair, Danilevsky said:

'Own up, colleague, you must have oriental blood in your veins. Would it be Jewish, perhaps, or Caucasian?'

With his unfailing alacrity, Levitsky replied:

'Absolutely not, Nikolay Grigorevich, there's not a drop of

Jewish blood in me. Polish, yes, and maybe a bit of Ukrainian like you – after all, there are some Ukrainian Levitskys – and my grandfather did tell me there might be a little Turkish, but whether that's true or not only Allah knows.'

And Danilevsky burst into delighted laughter.

'Well, there you are! I guessed right! Be on your guard, ladies and maidens, he's a Turk and not nearly as meek as you might suppose. And amorous too, in the Turkish fashion. Whose turn is it now, colleague? Who's the lady of your valiant heart at present?'

'Daria Tadiyevna,' Levitsky replied with an ingenuous smile, a swift clear flame suffusing his cheeks – he would often blush and smile like that.

Daria Tadiyevna, a handsome woman with bluish down on her upper lip and along her cheeks, and a little black silk cap on her head after a recent bout of typhus, was reclining in an armchair and also gave way to such charming confusion that her black-currant eyes all but disappeared for a moment.

'Well, that's hardly a secret, and perfectly understandable,' she said, 'after all, I too have oriental blood . . .'

And Grisha began to yell with glee: 'Got them, got them!', while Zoyka ran headlong into the next room and fell flat on her back against the edge of a sofa, her eyes squinting.

That winter Levitsky was in fact secretly in love with Daria Tadiyevna, having previously entertained certain sentiments towards Zoyka. Zoyka was only fourteen years old, but already very well developed physically, especially when viewed from behind, even though the bare, pearly-blue knees beneath her short tartan skirt were still childishly rounded and tender. A year ago she had been taken away from school and was not receiving any tuition at home – Danilevsky had discovered the symptoms of some kind of mental disorder in her – so she lived in a state of happy-go-lucky idleness, never bored. She was so caressing with everyone that she would actually lick her lips. Her forehead was domed, there was an expression of naïve, constantly surprised rapture in her glistening blue eyes, and her lips were always moist. In spite of the heaviness of her body there was something gracefully coquettish about her movements. The red bow tied in her nutbrown, shimmering hair made her particularly seductive. She would climb, without restraint, into Levitsky's lap – in all innocence, it seemed, as a child might – and was probably only too aware of what he was secretly obliged to suffer, cradling her weight and her fullness and softness, averting his eyes from the bare knees beneath her little checked skirt. Sometimes he could bear it no longer and, as if joking, would kiss her cheek, while she'd close her eyes and smile a languorous, mocking smile. On one occasion, binding him to the most dreadful secrecy, she told him something about her mother that she and no-one else in the whole world knew: Mama was in love with young Dr Titov! Mama was forty years old, but nevertheless slender as a girl and terribly young-looking, and the two of them, Mama and the doctor, were so tall and beautiful! Then Levitsky stopped paying her any attention – Daria Tadiyevna had begun to appear in the house. Zoyka seemed to grow more merry and carefree than ever, but she never took her eyes off either Daria or Levitsky and although she would often run up shrieking to embrace her, Zoyka hated Daria so much that when the latter fell ill with typhus, she spent every day waiting for glad tidings of her death from the hospital. Afterwards she waited for her departure and for the advent of summer when Levitsky, freed from his studies, would begin to come to the dacha on the Kazan road where the Danilevskys had spent the last three summers: in her way she was chasing after him on the sly.

And so summer came and he began to arrive every week for two or three days at a time. But then shortly afterwards, Papa's niece from Kharkov, Valeria Ostrogradskaya whom neither Zoyka nor Grishka had ever met, came to stay. Early one morning Levitsky was dispatched by rail to Moscow to meet her train at the Kursk Station, and when he returned from the station he was no longer riding his bicycle but sitting beside her in the cab, exhausted, hollow-eyed, and filled with a joyous agitation. It was obvious that he had fallen in love with her even before leaving the Kursk Station, and when he dragged her baggage down from the cart she was already ordering him around. However, after running up onto the porch to greet Mama, she immediately forgot all about him and proceeded to ignore him for the rest of the day. Zoyka found her impossible to understand – arranging her things in her room and later having lunch on the veranda, she either chattered incessantly or fell into a deep silence, lost in her own thoughts. But nevertheless, she was a genuine Ukrainian beauty! And Zoyka pestered her indefatigably:

'Have you brought leather boots with you, and a brocade kerchief? Will you put them on? Will you let me call you Valechka?'

But even without her Ukrainian finery she was lovely: strong and well-made, with thick dark hair and velvet brows that almost met in the middle, stern eyes the colour of black blood, a hot dark flush on her sunburnt face, gleaming teeth and full cherry mouth. Her hands were small, but also strong, and evenly tanned as if very slightly smoked. And what shoulders! And how the pink silken ribbons holding up her under-bodice glimmered upon them through the thin stuff of her white blouse! Her skirt was rather short and plain but it fitted her to perfection. Zoyka was so captivated that she didn't even begrudge her Levitsky, who stopped going into Moscow and never left Valeria's side, happy because she had made him her friend, begun to call him George, and kept him constantly at her beck and call. Then came the real hot summer days, guests arrived more frequently from Moscow, and Zoyka noticed that Levitsky had been dismissed and was now usually to be found sitting by Mama's side, helping to pick over the raspberries, while Valeria had fallen for Dr Titov with whom Mama, too, was secretly in love. In any case, something had happened to Valeria – when there were no guests in the house she no longer bothered to change out of one elegant blouse into another as had been her way, and would sometimes go around from morning to night in Mama's peignoir, with a look of disdain on her face. It was all frightfully interesting. Had she or had she not exchanged kisses with Levitsky before falling in love with Titov? Grishka swore that one day before lunch he'd seen her with Levitsky walking back from bathing along the avenue of spruces, a towel wrapped like a turban around her head, while Levitsky, tripping up over the wet bath-sheet he was dragging along for her, kept repeating something again and again until finally she had paused for a moment and he had grabbed her by the shoulders and kissed her on the lips.

'I squeezed behind one of the spruces and they didn't see me,' Grishka avowed hotly, his eyes starting out of his head, 'but I saw everything. She was fantastically beautiful, only red all over because it was still terribly hot and of course she'd overdone the bathing – after all she stays in the water for two hours and swims, I've seen this too, naked as a naiad . . . and there he was babbling away, just like a real Turk . . .'

Grishka swore on his honour, but he enjoyed inventing all manner of rubbish and Zoyka only half-believed him.

On Saturdays and Sundays, even in the morning, the trains arriving at the station from Moscow were always packed with weekend visitors coming to see the families in the dachas. On some days delightful showers of rain, drifting through sunlight, would fall upon the green carriages, washing them until they shone as new, while the white puffs of steam rising from the engine would seem especially soft, and the green tops of the slender, closely-spaced pines standing beyond the train showed extraordinarily high and round against the brilliant sky. The new arrivals would vie with one another for the horse-drawn cabs waiting on the hot trodden sand behind the station, and, full of

the joys of the countryside, would bowl along the sandy roads
which ran through the cuttings in the pine forest, beneath the
heavenly streamers floating above. It was the season of complete
country bliss in the forest which stretched as far as the eye could
see across the dry, gently undulating terrain. Taking their
Moscow friends for a walk, the occupants of the dachas would
remark that all the place lacked was bears and recite: 'Wild
strawberries and resin perfume the sombre wood', and their
voices echoing playfully, revel in their summer well-being and
their free, festive garb – the loose peasant shirts with embroidered
hems, long brightly-coloured corded belts and canvas caps: some
Moscow acquaintance, some bearded and bespectacled professor
or magazine editor, might not be instantly recognizable in shirts
and caps such as these.

Amid all this pastoral happiness, Levitsky was doubly miser-
able, feeling pitiful, betrayed, and in the way from morning to
night. Day and night the same thought churned in his brain:
why, oh why, had she so swiftly and so mercilessly attached him
to her side, first making him her half-friend, half-slave, and then a
lover who had to content himself with the rare, always unexp-
ected bliss of mere kisses; why did she sometimes address him in
the intimate singular and other times in the formal plural, and
how could she have found the cruelty to stop noticing his
existence with such ease and such simplicity from the very first
day of her acquaintance with Titov? He also burnt with shame at
the thought of the unscrupulous way he was hanging about the
place. He would have to disappear the very next day, flee in
secret to Moscow and hide away from everyone with this
shameful grief of betrayed country-house love, now so obvious
even to the servants! But at this thought he would be pierced by
such a vivid memory of her velvety cherry mouth that he lost all
power over his arms and legs. If he were sitting all alone on the
veranda when she happened to come strolling by, without
stopping and with excessive naturalness she would say something

particularly insignificant: 'Where is my aunt? Have you seen her?', and he would hasten to reply in the same tone, ready to sob aloud with pain. One day when she was passing by she saw him with Zoyka on his knee – what business was it of hers? But her eyes blazed with sudden fury and she gave a ringing cry: 'Don't you dare climb all over men's knees, you filthy little girl!' – and he was seized with joy: she was jealous, jealous! Meanwhile, Zoyka made the most of every available opportunity to trap him in some empty room where she could fling her arms around his neck, and, her eyes gleaming, licking her lips, whisper hastily: 'Sweetheart, sweetheart, sweetheart!' On one occasion she managed to catch his lips with her moist mouth so deftly that for the rest of the day he was unable to think of her without a bittersweet tremor – and horror: What's the matter with me! How can I look Nikolay Grigorevich and Klavdia Aleksandrovna in the face after this!

The grounds of the dacha, as on a country estate, were extensive. To the right of the entrance stood a big, empty stable with a hayloft above, and then a long servants' wing connected to the kitchen, with birch and lime trees peeping out from behind, while to the left, on the firm, bumpy ground, stood several old spreading pines, the grass between them occupied by swings and giant's footsteps, and further away, close to the wall of the forest, was a smooth croquet lawn. The house, also large, stood immediately facing the entrance; behind it lay a sizeable area of mixed garden and woodland and a magnificently sombre avenue of ancient spruces which led straight through this mélange from the rear balcony down to the bathing-place on the lake. And the hosts, with or without guests, always sat on the front veranda which was set back into the house and shaded from the sun. On this particular hot Sunday morning the only people sitting on the veranda were the mistress of the house and Levitsky. The morning, as always when they had company, seemed to be especially festive; many guests had arrived and the maids, sparkling in their new dresses, ran without cease to and fro across the courtyard between the house and the kitchen where hasty preparations were being made for lunch. There were five new arrivals: a dark-complexioned, jaundiced writer who, while always excessively strict and serious, had a passionate fondness for games of every kind; a short-legged professor who looked like Socrates and had recently, at the age of fifty, become the husband of his twenty-year-old pupil, a skinny blonde who had come with him; a very elegant little lady who on account of her diminutive stature and leanness, her evil temper and touchiness, had been nicknamed The Wasp; and finally Titov, whom Danilevsky had dubbed The Impudent Gentleman. Now all these guests, Valeria, and Danilevsky himself were in the transparent shade of the pine trees on the edge of the forest. Danilevsky sat in his chair smoking a cigar, the children, together with the writer and the professor's wife, were racing round and round the giant's footsteps, while the professor, Titov, Valeria and The Wasp darted about with mallets, hitting croquet balls, calling to each other, arguing and quarrelling. Levitsky sat listening with the lady of the house. When he made an attempt to join the others, Valeria immediately shooed him away – 'My aunt is all alone stoning the cherries, go and help her at once!' He smiled awkwardly, stood for a moment watching her as, mallet in hand, she bent over the croquet ball, her tussore skirt swinging above the taut calf muscles in their fine straw-coloured stockings and her breasts pressing, heavy and full, against the transparent blouse through which the tanned flesh of her rounded shoulders appeared to be slightly rosy from the pink straps of her camisole – and wandered slowly back to the veranda. He was particularly pitiful that morning, and his hostess, calm and composed as ever, with her youthful face and clear gaze, also listening with a hidden ache in her heart to the voices under the pines, kept looking at him out of the corner of her eye.

'Now we'll never get our hands clean', she said, poking a little gilt fork into a cherry with her blood-stained fingers. 'And you,

George, you always manage to get yourself into such a mess . . . My dear, why are you still in your jacket, it's so hot, you could perfectly well go around in just a shirt with a belt. And you haven't shaved for ten days . . .'

He knew that his hollow cheeks were covered by a reddish stubble, that his one and only white jacket was filthy from constant wear, that the trousers of his student's uniform were shiny and his shoes unpolished, he knew how hunched he was, sitting there with his narrow chest and hollow stomach, and answered blushing:

'You're right, you're right, Klavdia Aleksandrovna, I'm covered in bristles like an escaped convict, I've really let myself go, imposed shamelessly on your kindness; please, for God's sake, forgive me. I'll pull myself together this very day, especially as it's high time I went back to Moscow. I've outstayed my welcome and everyone must be sick of the sight of me. I'll leave without fail tomorrow. One of my friends has invited me to Mogilyov – he writes that it's a marvellously picturesque town . . .'

And he bent even lower over the table, hearing Titov's peremptory voice shouting at Valeria:

'No, no, dear lady, that's not in the rules! If you don't know how to place your foot on the ball and end up hitting yourself with the mallet, that's your look-out – you're certainly not going to be allowed to croquet twice!'

At lunch, he felt as if all those sitting at the table had somehow got inside him and were eating, talking, making jokes and laughing there. After lunch everyone went off to rest in the shade of the spruces on the avenue, which was thickly carpeted with slippery pine needles; the maids had dragged out rugs and cushions. He walked across the baking courtyard to the empty stable, climbed the outside ladder into the semi-darkness of the loft, flung himself down on the musty hay which covered the floor, and lying on his stomach trying to reach some kind of decision, began to stare intently at a fly sitting on the hay immediately in front of his eyes; it first rubbed its front legs together in a rapid criss-cross motion as if washing its face, and then somehow, in defiance of nature, started with an effort to raise its hind ones. Suddenly, someone ran swiftly up into the loft, threw open the door and slammed it behind them – and turning round, in the light from the dormer window, he saw Zoyka. She jumped and sank into the hay beside him, and lying flat on her stomach too, panting, looking into his eyes as if scared, whispered:

'Georgik, sweetheart, I have something to tell you, something you'll find very interesting – something wonderful!'

'What is it, Zoyechka?' he asked, raising himself a little.

'You'll see! But first you have to give me a kiss for it, you absolutely have to!'

And she began to thrash her legs up and down in the hay, baring her plump thighs.

'Zoyechka,' he began, too weary from his emotional sufferings to resist a painful wave of tenderness. 'Zoyechka, you're the only one who loves me and I love you too, very much, but we mustn't, we mustn't . . .'

She thrashed her legs harder than ever.

'Yes, we must, we absolutely must!'

And she fell with her head on his breast. He saw her young, shining nutbrown hair beneath the red bow, inhaled its fragrance and pressed his face against it. Suddenly she gave a low, piercing 'Ow!' and grabbed the back of her skirt.

He leapt up.

'What is it?'

Throwing herself head-first into the hay, she burst into tears.

'I've been terribly stung, there . . . Look, please look, quickly!'

And she tossed her skirt over her back and tugged the knickers off her plump body.

'What can you see? Blood?'

'There's absolutely nothing, Zoyechka!'

'What do you mean, nothing?' she cried, bursting into tears again. 'Blow on it, blow on it, it's horribly painful!'

And having blown on it, he kissed the cool abundance of her wide, soft rear, greedily several times. She jumped up, wildly jubilant, eyes and teardrops glittering:

'Tricked you, tricked you, tricked you! And for that I'll tell you a most dreadful secret: Titov has given her her marching orders, her full marching orders! Grishka and I heard everything from behind the drawing-room chairs: they were walking up and down the veranda while we went and sat there on the floor behind the chairs and, terribly insultingly, he told her: "Dear lady, I'm not someone you can lead around on a string. Furthermore, I don't love you. I might one day, if and when you deserve it, but until then – no declarations!" Not bad, eh? Serves her right!'

And leaping to her feet she rushed to the door and down the ladder.

He gazed after her:

'I'm a scoundrel, hanging's too good for me!' he said out loud, the taste of her body still on his lips.

In the evening, the house grew quiet and a feeling of peace and of family privacy descended – the guests had driven away at six o'clock. Warm evening shadows and the medicinal scent of the lime trees flowering behind the kitchen. The sweet smell of smoke and of something cooking coming from the kitchen itself, where supper was being prepared. And the serene joy of all this – the twilight, the smells – and the torment of her presence which still seemed to hold some kind of promise, her continuing existence beside him . . . the soul-destroying torment of his love for her and her relentless indifference, absence . . . Where was she? He stepped down from the front veranda, listening to the rhythmic, regular sound of the swing screeching and creaking beneath the pine trees, and made his way towards it – yes, there she was. He stopped, watching her flying up and down in a wide arc, pulling harder and harder on the ropes, trying to rise to the uttermost point and pretending that she hadn't seen him. With a screech of the rings, she soared terrifyingly up and up to disappear into the branches before plummeting earthwards again as if someone had shot her down, flexing her knees, the hem of her dress billowing. Oh if only he could catch her, strangle her, ravish her!

'Valeria Andreyevna! Take care!'

As if she hadn't heard him, she swung higher still . . .

At supper on the veranda, they laughed at the guests, arguing about them. Unnaturally and spitefully, she laughed too, gobbling curd cheese and sour cream, again without a single glance in his direction. Only Zoyka said nothing and kept looking at him out of the corner of an eye that glittered with a knowledge he alone shared.

They all went off to bed early, and there wasn't a single light left in the house. Everywhere was dark and lifeless. Having unobtrusively slipped away to his room, the door of which gave onto the veranda, straight after supper, he began to cram his few scraps of linen into a rucksack, thinking: 'I'll take my bicycle out without making a sound, jump on it – and off to the station! I'll lie down on the sand somewhere in the forest near the station and wait for the first morning train . . .' Or no, that wouldn't do. God knows how it would look . . . He ran away like a little boy in the middle of the night, without saying goodbye to anyone! Best wait until tomorrow and leave casually, as if nothing had happened: 'Goodbye, dear Nikolay Grigorevich, goodbye dear Klavdia Aleksandrovna. Many, many thanks for everything! Yes, I'm off to Mogilyov, they say it's an amazingly beautiful town . . . Look after yourself, Zoyechka my dear, keep on growing and be happy! Grisha, let me shake you by the hand. Valeria Andreyevna, all the best, no hard feelings . . .' No, the 'hard feelings' were a bad idea, stupid and tactless, as if he were hinting at something . . .

Realizing that he didn't have the slightest hope of going to sleep, he stepped quietly down from the veranda and decided to try and relax a little by walking three versts or so down the road leading to the station. But when he reached the courtyard, he paused: the warm shadows and the delicious silence, the milky pallor of the sky with its countless tiny stars . . . He walked on across the courtyard and paused again, throwing back his head: the firmament was retreating further and further into the vault above him where there was a frightening blue-black darkness, and chasms opening into he knew not where . . . And oh, the peace, the silence, the incomprehensible grandeur of that void, the lifeless, pointless beauty of the world, the mute, eternal religiousness of the night . . . He was alone, face to face with it all, lost in the abyss between earth and sky. And he began to pray wordlessly, deep inside his being, for some kind of celestial mercy, for someone to take pity on him, feeling with a bitter joy that he was at one with the heavens and that he had already, somehow, been released from the burden of himself, of his body . . . Then trying not to lose this feeling, he turned and looked back at the house: the stars swam, flattened, in the black glass of the window panes – and in the glass of her window as well . . . Was she sleeping or lying awake in the leaden torpor of her obsession with Titov? Yes, now it was her turn.

He circled the big house lying indistinct in the shadows and walked towards the rear balcony and the grassy patch that stretched between it and the double row of motionless spruces which towered black and menacing against the night, their pointed tops touching the stars. The unblinking, greeny-yellow lights of the fireflies studded the darkness beneath the spruces. And on the balcony there was the faint glimmer of something white. He paused and all of a sudden gave a start of terror and surprise – a quiet, even and expressionless voice reached him from the balcony.

'What are you doing, wandering around at night?'

Amazed, he took a step forward and at once made her out: she was reclining in a rocking-chair, enveloped in the old-fashioned silvery shawl which was worn in the evening by any female Danilevsky guest who happened to stay the night. In his confusion, he too asked her a question:

'Why aren't you asleep?'

She didn't reply, remaining silent for a moment, then stood up and glided noiselessly down to where he was standing, shrugging the shawl back onto her shoulders.

'Let's walk a little . . .'

He followed her, a few steps behind to begin with and then by her side, into the darkness of the avenue which seemed to be hiding something in its motionless gloom. What was happening? He was alone with her again, just the two of them, in this avenue and at this late hour? And the shawl, which as usual was sliding from her shoulders, pricked the tips of his fingers with its little silken hairs when he straightened it about her . . . Controlling the spasm in his throat, he said:

'Why – for what possible reason – must you torture me so?'

She shook her head.

'I don't know. Be quiet.'

Feeling a little bolder, he raised his voice.

'Yes, why and for what possible reason – why did you have to –'

She caught the hand that was dangling at his side and squeezed it:

'Be quiet!'

'Valya, I don't understand anything . . .'

She let go of his hand and glanced to the left, towards the spruce which stood spreading the broad triangle of its dark mantle at the end of the avenue.

'Do you remember this spot? This is where I kissed you that first time. Now kiss me here for the last time . . .'

And passing rapidly under the branches of the tree, she threw the shawl impetuously to the ground.

'Come to me!'

As soon as the final moment had passed, she thrust him away from her brutally and with loathing, and apart from lowering her raised and parted knees and allowing her arms to drop to her sides, remained where she was. He lay spreadeagled on the ground beside her with his face pressed against the pine needles, scalding them with his tears. In the chill silence of the night and the forest, glowing red in the distance like a motionless slice of melon above the dim fields, was the lingering moon.

Back in his room, he glanced at his watch with tear-swollen eyes and became afraid: it was twenty to two! Hastily, trying not to make a sound, he wheeled his bicycle down from the veranda and pushed it quickly and noiselessly across the courtyard. On the other side of the gates, he leapt into the saddle and hunched low over the handle-bars pedalled furiously away, bouncing over the sandy pot-holes of the cutting between the serried ranks of black tree-trunks which came rushing towards him from both sides, flickering against the pre-dawn sky. 'I'll be late!' And he pedalled more furiously than ever, wiping the sweat from his brow with the crook of his arm: the Moscow mail-train flew through the station without stopping at 2.15, so he had only a few minutes left. Suddenly, at the end of the cutting, in the dawn's half-light which still seemed like dusk, he saw the dark shape of the station. Now for it! He turned resolutely to the left along the road which ran parallel to the railway tracks, then to the right, passing under the barrier to the level crossing, then again to the left between the rails, and raced clattering over the sleepers to the foot of the gradient, towards the roar and blinding lights of the locomotive that burst over the top.

13 October 1940

The Riverside Tavern

Translated by David Richards

In the Prague Restaurant the chandeliers were glittering, the music of a Portuguese string orchestra blended with the noise of dining and conversation, and there wasn't a single free place. I stood for a moment looking round and was just about to go away when I caught sight of an army doctor of my acquaintance who immediately invited me to join him at his table by a window which opened onto the warm spring night and the Arbat with its roaring trams. We dined together and drank a fair amount of vodka and Cahetian wine while talking about the recently convened state Duma, then we ordered coffee. The doctor took out an old silver cigar-case, offered me his Asmolov 'cannon', and said as he lit up:

'Yes, it's all Duma, Duma. Shouldn't we have a drop of brandy? It all makes me feel sad somehow.'

He was a placid, rather dry fellow with a firm, strong figure that fitted well into military uniform, and wiry red hair greying at the temples. I took his words as a joke, but he added seriously:

'It must be the spring that makes me sad. As you get older, especially if you're a bachelor and a dreamer, you become generally much more sensitive then when you were young. Can you smell the poplars, and can you hear the trams roaring? . . . But let's shut the window; it's rather uncomfortable,' he said, standing up. 'Ivan Stepanych, some Shustovskoye brandy, please.'

While the old waiter was fetching the Shustovskoye, the doctor sat in an absent-minded silence. When a glass had been poured out for each of us he kept the bottle on the table and continued sipping the brandy from a small hot cup as well.

'Now here's something for you – a few memories. Just before you arrived, Bryusov the poet called in here with a thin little thing who looked like a poverty-stricken student. In that barking nasal burr of his he shouted a few short, sharp, angry words at the head waiter who'd run up obviously to apologize for the lack of places – they must have been booked by telephone but not kept – and then haughtily withdrew. You know him well, but I know something of him too, I come across him in old Russian icon circles – I've been interested in icons for a long time now, in the ones from the towns along the Volga where I once served for several years. Besides that, I've also heard a good deal about him, about his affairs, amongst other things, so I felt a certain pity for that girl who was clearly his latest admirer and victim. There was something terribly touching about her as she looked, with dismay and excitement, first at this dazzling restaurant, which she was probably not at all used to, and then at him as he uttered his preposterous bark, demonically rolling his black eyes and flutter-ing his eyelashes. It was all that that brought back my memories. I'll tell you one of them, the one that scene brought to mind, now the orchestra's going off and we can sit here quietly for a while . . .'

His face was already flushed with the vodka, the Cahetian wine and the brandy – in the way red-haired people always become red from wine – but he poured out another glass for each of us.

'I recalled,' he began, 'how one day twenty years ago, walking through the streets of a certain town on the Volga was a young army doctor, that is, to put it bluntly, myself. I was walking along on a trifling errand, I remember to post some letter, with that carefree feeling of well-being in my heart which we some-times experience for no reason at all in good weather. And the weather really was beautiful; it was one of those quiet, dry, sunny evenings in early September when the fallen leaves on the

pavement rustle so pleasantly under your feet. And so, not
thinking about anything in particular, I raise my eyes and see
hurrying along ahead of me a very slender, elegant girl in a grey
suit and a little grey beautifully shaped hat, and carrying a grey
umbrella in a hand cased in an olive-green suede glove. I see her
and sense that there is something terribly attractive about her and
yet also something that seems rather strange. Why and where is
she walking so quickly? It wouldn't seem there's anything to be
surprised about – people have lots of urgent business, don't they?
But all the same, somehow it intrigues me. Unconsciously I
increase my own pace and almost catch up with her – as it turns
out, not in vain. Ahead on a corner stands a little, low, ancient
church, and I see her going straight towards it, though it's a
weekday and a time when there aren't any services on. She runs
into the porch and with an effort opens the heavy door; I do the
same behind her, go in, but stop just inside the door. The church
is empty and, not seeing me, she walks with a quick light step up
to the pulpit, crosses herself and sinks gracefully to her knees,
throws back her head and, dropping the umbrella on the floor,
clasps her hands to her bosom and stares at the altar, everything
about her emphasizing that insistently beseeching gaze with
which people beg for God's help in great sorrow or when they
have a fervent desire for something. Through the narrow,
iron-grilled window to my left comes a yellowish evening light,
peaceful, wistful and also somehow of another age, while in front
of me the vaulted interior of the squat church is already gloomy,
with just a flicker of light coming from the gold frames of the
altar-wall icons which had been forged with a wonderful ancient
roughness; and she, on her knees, doesn't take her eyes off them.
A slender waist, a lyre back, and the little heels of her light,
elegant shoes with their toes digging into the floor . . . Then she
dabs her eyes several times with a little handkerchief, quickly
picks up the umbrella as if she's suddenly formed a resolve,
lightly gets up, runs towards the exit, suddenly sees my face –

and I'm simply staggered by the beauty of the most dreadful look of terror which flashes in her bright, tear-filled eyes . . .'

In the next room a chandelier was extinguished – the restaurant was already empty – and the doctor glanced at his watch.

'It isn't late yet,' he said. 'Only ten. You're not in a hurry? Well, then, let's sit here a little longer and I'll tell you the end of this rather odd story. The odd thing about it was that on that very same evening, or rather, late that evening, I met her again. I'd suddenly taken it into my head to go to a summer-season tavern on the Volga which I'd visited not more than two or three times that whole summer and then only in order to sit for a while in the river air after a hot day in the town. Why precisely I went there that cool evening, God only knows: it was as if something guided me there. You could of course say it was simply chance – a man goes somewhere because he has nothing to do and there's nothing surprising if a second chance meeting occurs. Of course, that's all perfectly true. But why then was there something more, how did it come about that I met her again in that wretched place and suddenly those vague speculations and presentiments which I'd experienced when I first saw her were confirmed, that concentration and mysterious anxious purposefulness with which she'd entered the church and there prayed to God so intensely and silently, with the most important and most genuine part of herself? When I arrived I'd completely forgotten about her and sat for a long time alone and bored in that riverside tavern – which incidentally was very expensive and well known for the extravagant nocturnal junketings it used to put on for merchants – sipping a glass of Zhiguli beer without much pleasure, recalling the Rhine and the Swiss lakes where I'd been the previous summer and thinking how vulgar all Russian provincial places for out-of-town entertainment are, particularly along the Volga. Have you been to those Volga towns, to taverns like that, standing on piles over the water?'

I replied that I hardly knew the Volga and had never been in the restaurants on the water, but could easily imagine them.

'Well, of course,' he said, 'the Russian provinces are pretty much the same everywhere. There's only one thing in them that's quite unique, and that's the Volga itself. From early spring right up to winter it is always and everywhere extraordinary, in all weathers and whether it's day or night. At night you can sit, for instance, in a tavern like that one and look out of the windows which form three of its walls, and when they are all open to the air on a summer night you look straight into the darkness, into the blackness of the night, and somehow you sense especially keenly all the wild magnificence of the watery wastes outside; you see thousands of bright-coloured lights, you hear the splash of passing rafts and the voices of the peasants on the rafts and the barges and the wherries, shouting warnings to each other; you hear the varied music of the steamers' sirens, first booming, then low and, merging with that, the notes of the fast-running river-boats; you recall all those brigand and Tartar names – Balakhna, Vasilsursk, Cheboksary, Zhiguli, Batraki, Khvalynsk – and the great hordes of dockers on their jetties, then all the incomparable beauty of the ancient Volga churches . . . and all you can do is shake your head. Indeed, is there anything to compare with this Old Russia of ours? But then you look round and ask what, if we're honest about it, is this tavern? A structure on wooden piles, a log barn with windows in crude frames, packed with tables hidden under grubby white table-cloths, with cheap heavy cutlery, where the salt in the salt-cellars is mixed with pepper and the napkins smell of cheap soap; you see a platform of planks, a farcical stage for balalaika-players, accordionists and lady harpists, illuminated along its back wall by kerosene lamps with their blinding tin reflectors; you see yellow-haired waiters, a landlord of peasant stock with thick hair and little bear-like eyes – and how can you reconcile all this with the fact that again and again a thousand roubles' worth of Mumm and Roederer is drunk in one night! All that is Old Russia too, you know. But am I boring you?'

'Certainly not,' I said.

'Well, then, let me finish my story. This is all leading up to showing what a foul place it was where I suddenly met her again in all her pure noble charm, and in what company! Towards midnight the tavern began to get more lively and to fill up; the huge, dreadfully bright light on the ceiling was lit, and the wall-lights and the little lights behind the platform; a whole regiment of waiters emerged and a crowd of clients flocked in – merchants' sons of course, officials, contractors, steamship captains, a troupe of actors on tour in the town . . . The waiters ran around with trays, bending lasciviously, from the parties at the tables came loud words and laughter, tobacco smoke drifted about; some balalaika-players in stage-peasant shirts, fresh socks and new bast shoes came out onto the platform and sat in two rows along the sides, to be followed by a choir of rouged and powdered whores who stood in a line with their hands uniformly placed behind their backs and joined the twanging balalaikas with shrill voices and blank faces in a doleful, long-drawn-out song about some unhappy 'warrior' who seemed to have returned from a lengthy captivity in Turkey:

> "For his loved ones knew him n-o-ot,
> And asked him who he wa-a-as . . ."

Then a certain "celebrated Ivan Grachov" came on with a huge accordion, sat on a stool at the very front of the platform, and tossed his thick flaxen hair with its loutish middle parting; he had a cleaner's face, and wore a yellow shirt embroidered in red silk across the high collar and the hem, a braided red belt with long frayed edges hanging down, and new boots with patent-leather tops. He tossed his hair, placed the three-tiered accordion with its black and gold bellows on his raised knee, fixed his pewter-coloured eyes on some point aloft, essayed a devil-may-care run over the keys and then began to make them growl and chant as he wrung and twisted and stretched the bellows like a fat snake, running his fingers over the keys with astonishing flourishes and ever-increasing volume, boldness and variety – then he suddenly threw back his head, shut his eyes and poured forth in a feminine voice:

> "I walked in the meadows,
> To banish my sorrow . . ."

It was at that very moment I suddenly caught sight of her, and of course not her alone. At that exact moment I'd stood up in order to call the waiter and pay for my beer – and I found myself gasping in surprise: a door behind the platform had opened from outside and she appeared, wearing some sort of little khaki peaked cap, and a belted raincoat of the same colour – truly, she looked astonishingly good in those things, like a tall boy – and behind her, holding her by the elbow, was a short fellow in a light coat and a nobleman's cap, with a dark, prematurely lined face and black, restless eyes. And, you know, as the saying goes, you could have knocked me down with a feather! I recognized in him an acquaintance of mine, a spendthrift landowner, a drunkard and a debauchee, a former lieutenant in the hussars who'd been cashiered, and without stopping to think, I rushed through the tables so impulsively that I reached the two of them still almost at the entrance. Ivan Grachov was bawling:

> "I looked for a flower,
> To give to my love . . ."

As I ran up to them he glanced at me and managed to exclaim cheerily: "Ah, good evening, doctor," while she turned as pale as death, but I pushed him aside and whispered to her furiously: "You – in this tavern! At midnight, with a debauched drunkard and cheat, a man notorious throughout the district!" I seized her by the arm, threatening to do him an injury unless she left with me that very minute. He stood rooted to the spot – what else could he do, knowing that with these hands of mine I can break horseshoes? She turned, lowered her head and walked towards the exit. I caught her up under the first lamp-post on the cobbled embankment and took her arm. She didn't raise her head or free her arm. At the second lamp-post, beside a bench, she stopped and, leaning against me, shuddered and burst into tears. I sat her on the bench, took her tear-stained, sweet slim girlish hand in mine and put my other arm round her shoulders. She was babbling incoherently: "No, it's not true, it's not true. He's good . . . he's unhappy, but he's kind, generous and easy-going . . ." I remained silent. There was no point in trying to object. Then I hailed a passing cab. She calmed down and we drove up into the town in silence. In the square she said softly: "Now let me go. I'll walk home. I don't want you to know where I live." And quickly kissing my hand, she jumped down and without looking round set off uncertainly, diagonally across the square. I never saw her again, and to this day I still don't know who or what she was.'

When we'd settled our bills, put on our coats downstairs and gone out, the doctor walked with me to the corner of the Arbat where we stopped to say goodbye. The streets were empty and quiet, awaiting fresh activity towards midnight when people would be coming out of the theatres and from the restaurants in and outside the city. The sky was black, the street lights gleamed brightly under the elegant fresh foliage on Prechistensky Boulevard, and there was a soft smell of spring rain which had moistened the roadway while we were sitting in the Prague.

'But do you know,' said the doctor, glancing round, 'later I regretted that I'd, so to speak, saved her. I've met other cases of that sort. Why, I must ask, did I interfere? Does it matter how or why someone is happy? After-effects? For you know one way or another there always are after-effects – everything leaves cruel traces in the heart, memories, I mean, which are particularly cruel and agonizing when you remember something happy . . . Well, good-bye, it was nice seeing you . . .'

27 October 1943

A Cold Autumn

Translated by David Richards

In June of that year he was staying with us on the estate. He'd always been considered one of us, as his late father had been a friend and neighbour of my father's. On the fifteenth of June Franz Ferdinand was killed in Sarajevo. On the morning of the sixteenth the newspapers were delivered from the post office. Father emerged from his study carrying a Moscow evening paper and entered the dining-room, where he, Mama and I were still sitting at the table, and said:

'Well, my friends, it's war! The Austrian Crown-Prince has been killed in Sarajevo. It's war!'

On St Peter's Day a crowd of visitors gathered at the house – it was father's name-day – and over dinner our engagement was announced. But on the nineteenth of July Germany declared war on Russia.

In September he came to us for just twenty-four hours, to say goodbye before going off to the front. (Everyone at that time thought that the war would soon be over, and our wedding had been postponed till the spring). So this was our last evening together. After supper the servants brought in the samovar as usual and as he glanced at the windows which were steamed up from its heat, father said:

'What an astonishingly early and cold autumn!'

We sat quietly that evening, only occasionally exchanging the odd insignificant word, hiding our innermost thoughts and feelings with exaggerated calm. It was with the same affected simplicity that father had made his remark about the autumn. I went up to the door onto the balcony and wiped the glass with a cloth: out in the garden the pure icy stars were sparkling with a sharp brilliance against the black sky. Father was smoking, leaning back in his armchair and absently gazing at the hot lamp suspended over the table; by its light Mama, in her spectacles, was carefully sewing a little silk bag – we knew what it was for – and the scene was both touching and chilling.

Father asked:

'So, you still want to set off in the morning rather than after lunch?'

'Yes, if I may, in the morning,' he answered. 'It's very sad, but I still haven't quite managed to see to everything at home.'

Father let out a slight sigh:

'Well, as you wish, dear boy. Only in that case it's time Mama and I went to bed; we certainly don't want to miss seeing you off tomorrow . . .'

Mama stood up and made the sign of the cross over her son to be; he bent down and kissed her hand, and then father's. Left alone, we lingered in the dining-room; I decided to set out a game of patience, while he paced from one corner of the room to another. Then suddenly he asked:

'Shall we go for a little walk?'

My heart was growing heavier and heavier, and I answered indifferently:

'All right.'

As he put on his coat in the entrance hall he was still deep in thought, and then with a sweet smile he suddenly recited some lines from Fet:

> 'What a cold autumn!
> Put on your bonnet and shawl . . .'

'I don't have a bonnet,' I said. 'But how does it go on?'

'I don't remember. Something like:

'Look – through the darkening pine-trees
A fire is arising . . .'

'What fire?'

'The rising moon, of course. There's a certain autumnal, rustic charm in those lines: "Put on your bonnet and shawl." That's our grandfathers' and grandmothers' time . . . Oh, my God, my God!'

'What is it?'

'Nothing, dearest love. But I do feel sad. Sad, but contented. I love you very, very much . . .'

We put our coats on, went through the dining-room out onto the balcony and then down into the garden. At first it was so dark I held onto his sleeve. Then the black boughs which were sprinkled with metallically brilliant stars began to stand out against the lightening sky. Stopping for a moment, he turned to face the house:

'Look how the windows are shining in a special autumn way. I shall remember this evening as long as I live.'

I looked at the windows, and he embraced me in my Swiss cloak. I brushed my mohair scarf away from my face and tilted my head back slightly so he could kiss me. When he'd kissed me he looked into my face.

'How your eyes sparkle,' he said. 'Aren't you cold? The air's quite wintry. If I'm killed, you won't forget me straightaway?'

I found myself thinking: 'Suppose he really is killed? Surely there won't come a time when I'll forget him – though in the end we do forget everything . . .'

And frightened by my own thought, I answered hurriedly:

'Don't talk like that. I wouldn't survive your death.'

After a short pause he pronounced slowly:

'Anyway, if I am killed, I'll wait for you over there. You live, be happy for a while in the world, and then come to me.'

I burst into tears . . .

In the morning he set off. Round his neck Mama hung that
fateful little bag she'd been sewing the previous evening – it
contained a small golden icon which had been carried to war by
both her father and her grandfather – and we made the sign of the
cross over him with nervously jerky despair. Watching him go,
we stood on the porch in that state of stupefaction always
experienced when saying farewell to someone before a long
separation, and all we felt was the astonishing incongruity
between ourselves and the joyful, sunny morning around us with
its hoar-frost sparkling on the grass. We stood there for a while
and then went back into the house. I walked through the rooms
with my hands behind my back, not knowing what to do with
myself, whether I should sob or sing at the top of my voice . . .

He was killed – what a strange word! – a month later, in
Galicia. And since then a whole thirty years have passed. And
I've experienced so much through those years which seem so long
when you consider them carefully and go over in your memory
all that magical, incomprehensible thing called the past which
neither the mind nor the heart can grasp. In the spring of 1918,
by which time my father and mother were both dead, I was living
in Moscow, in the cellar of a house belonging to a woman trading
in the Smolensk market who regularly mocked me with her 'Well,
your excellency, how are your circumstances?' I engaged in trade
myself and, like many others at that time, I sold to soldiers in
Caucasian fur caps and unbuttoned greatcoats some of the things
I still had – a ring, a little cross, a moth-eaten fur collar – and then
one day while trading on the corner of the Arbat and the
Smolensk market I met a man with a rare beautiful soul, an
elderly retired soldier; we soon got married and in April I went
off with him to Yekaterinodar. It took almost two weeks to get
there with him and his nephew, a boy of seventeen who was
trying to make his way to the Volunteers – I disguised as a
peasantwoman in bast shoes, he in a worn Cossack coat and with
a newly-grown black and silver beard – and then we spent over

two years on the Don and in the Kuban. In the winter, during a hurricane, we set sail from Novorossiysk for Turkey with a huge crowd of other refugees, and on the way, at sea, my husband died of typhus. After that, of all my nearest and dearest only three remained in the whole world – my husband's nephew, the latter's wife and their little girl, a child of seven months. But soon after this the nephew sailed off with his wife for the Crimea to join up with Wrangel, leaving the child on my hands. There they too disappeared without trace. And then I lived for a long time in Constantinople, earning a living for myself and the child by back-breaking manual labour. Then, like so many others, I wandered the world with her – Bulgaria, Serbia, Bohemia, Belgium, Paris, Nice . . . The little girl grew up long ago; she stayed in Paris and became a model Frenchwoman, very pretty and completely indifferent to me; she used to work in a confectioner's near the Madeleine, using her manicured hands with their silver fingernails to wrap up boxes in satin paper and gold string; and I lived, and am still living in Nice on what God provides . . . I saw Nice for the first time in 1912 – and could never have imagined in those happy days what the city would one day become for me!

So I did survive his death, even though I once impetuously said I wouldn't. But when I recall everything I've experienced since that time, I always ask myself: 'What, when all is said and done, has there been in my life?' And I answer: 'Only that cold autumn evening.' Did it ever exist? Yes, it did. And that is all there's been in my life. All the rest has been a useless dream. But I believe, I do ardently believe that somewhere over there he is waiting for me – with the same love and the same youthfulness as on that evening. 'You live, be happy for a while in the world, and then come to me . . .' I have lived, I have been happy for a while, and now, quite soon, I'll come.

3 May 1944

Also published by Angel Books

NIKOLAY LESKOV
Five Tales
Translated by Michael Shotton

FYODOR DOSTOYEVSKY
The Village of Stepanchikovo
Translated by Ignat Avsey

ALEXANDER PUSHKIN
The Tales of Belkin
with The History of the Village of Goryukhino
Translated by Gillon Aitken and David Budgen

ALEXANDER PUSHKIN
Mozart and Salieri
The 'Little Tragedies' translated by Antony Wood

AFANASY FET
I Have Come to You to Greét You
*Selected poems translated by James Greene
with essays by Henry Gifford and Yevgeny Vinokurov*

In preparation

VSEVOLOD GARSHIN
From the Reminiscences of Private Ivanov
and other stories translated by Peter Henry and Liv Tudge

JOHANN WOLFGANG VON GOETHE
Torquato Tasso
Translated by Alan Brownjohn

LUDWIG TIECK, HEINRICH VON KLEIST
and E.T.A. HOFFMANN
Five German Romantic Tales
Translated by Ronald Taylor